# Teamwork

*Gordon and Rosemary Jones*

**Scripture Union**
130 City Road, London EC1V 2NJ

# Contents

# Preface

This book has arisen out of work with Wycliffe Bible Translators. Their goal is to give the Bible to those who, as yet, do not have the Bible in their own mother tongue. There are nearly 6,000 Wycliffe members working in over fifty countries. We have developed these teambuilding materials while trying to help Wycliffe people work together on their assignments.

Throughout nearly thirty years in Christian service we have worked very closely together, having a joint ministry. This book is a product of our joint experience and different gifts. For the sake of clarity it is sometimes written in the first person.

All our work follows the rules of confidentiality observed in counselling work and for this reason the real-life illustrations given have been modified so that the 'clients' are not identifiable. The type of work they were engaged in, the country they worked in, even their gender, may have been changed in order to maintain their anonymity. However, they are based on actual people with whom we have worked, either in Wycliffe or in the local church.

# Acknowledgements

This book is a team effort. Neither of us feel that, individually, we are able to write. Together, with a much broader range of gifts, it's possible.

Our thanks to Docco, Bonni, Di, Judith, Philip, Andy, Jenny, Elizabeth, Trevis, Joy and Pam, who commented on the manuscript at various stages and gave us feedback. Many other friends and colleagues also read through the manuscript for us. In particular, Joyce Dibb did considerable editing. It was truly a team effort.

Our thanks to those who have stood with us in our Wycliffe work for nearly thirty years. Without their support and prayers we should not have been able to do it. In particular, we would like to thank our supporting churches of Holy Trinity, Redhill, St Andrew's, High Wycombe and St Mary's, Aldridge.

**Gordon and Rosemary Jones**

# 1

# A desert experience

An American missionary couple, with teenage children, were working as Bible translators among a North American Indian group in Arizona. They had been living and working there for more than twenty years. Our year-long assignment was to go out to help them. We were a young British couple with three small children, whose cross-cultural experience was virtually nil. All of us had to live together in one mobile home in the middle of the Arizona desert – what a scenario for possible miscommunication!

## Different expectations

Our first mistake was in our expectations. We had expected Americans to think and react as we do, even to share our sense of humour. They don't. We had expected to be told what to do, to be given a job description, or at least given a very specific part of the task as ours. We weren't.

We had also expected to live in a separate caravan, and lead a planned, fairly ordered family life as we did at home. We couldn't. We had been used to sharing our home with others, but it was *our* home we were sharing. We had been in control, 'calling the shots'. Now we were sharing someone else's home. We had lost control.

We were under considerable stress. Our background and that of our colleagues differed greatly. Our values, temperaments and interests were also very different. We knew little about white American culture and values and almost nothing about American Indians. One of the biggest hurdles lay in the whole area of communication. Looking back, we don't think we did a very good job in communicating our feelings and our needs. Probably we didn't do a very good job of understanding the feelings and needs of our colleagues, either.

We had both lost our roles. Rosemary had been used to running a home, organising the family and having a job at the British Wycliffe Centre. Suddenly all that had gone. Gordon had lost his role too. He had been used to being the manager of the Wycliffe Centre, with about twenty people working for him. His days in England had been filled to the brim with bustle. How was he to spend his time now? What could he achieve that was really worthwhile? We did not have the experience, knowledge or maturity to understand what was happening to us, nor what to do about it.

## What did we do?

Often we would go for a walk in the desert, sit down and pray, ask the Lord to help us, and try to plan a strategy together. That helped us, drew us closer together as a couple and kept us reliant on the Lord. What didn't we do? We didn't sit down with our colleagues and share our feelings. We didn't agree goals and a timetable to work towards these goals.

Many years have gone by since then. Now we are involved in helping other Wycliffe members in similar, often even more challenging situations to operate together and to be good teams.

## Closeness isn't easy

When we live and work very closely together, relationships can be particularly difficult. In the local church, where members lead separate working lives and live in houses some distance apart, the stresses are lessened, but even then there can be considerable friction.

When people share an apartment, or are in some other

communal living situation, it is often a source of strain. In overseas Christian work team members often live, work and relax together in very close proximity. Most of us would find our closest friendships tested if we had to live under such conditions.

## We expect too much

Even when we don't live together, simply working together can be stressful. In any kind of Christian work our expectations are high. If we are tackling a job in the local church, or entering 'full time' Christian service, we are highly motivated and therefore ready to invest a large amount of emotional energy. And if, when we throw ourselves into such work expecting much in return, we are thwarted or frustrated, we can react very strongly.

Christians are often more tolerant of unbelievers than of fellow Christians, because we expect other Christians to be able to obey the Bible's commands. One leader said that he felt the high standards we set each other are one of the reasons why Christians sometimes have difficulty working together. Yet the Bible assumes human frailty, weakness and sin. God is more understanding of our shortcomings than we are of each other's!

## The Bible teaches teamwork

The Bible lays considerable emphasis on togetherness, which suggests that there are many spiritual benefits of teamwork. In the New Testament alone, there are more than forty different verses that tell us how to relate to each other (see Exercise 1, page 160). We were created to be dependent on God, but also interdependent with one another.

In the Old Testament also, there are inspiring accounts of teamwork on spiritual and physical tasks – the rebuilding of the walls of Jerusalem under Nehemiah's leadership is just one example. Ecclesiastes, one of the 'wisdom' books, leaves us in no doubt that teamwork pays.

> Two are better than one, because they have a good
> return for their work:
> If one falls down, his friend can help him up.
> But pity the man who falls and has no-one to help
> him up!
> Also, if two lie down together, they will keep warm.
> But how can one keep warm alone?
> Though one may be overpowered, two can defend
> themselves.
> A cord of three strands is not quickly broken.
>
> *Ecclesiastes 4:9–12*

This doesn't deny our uniqueness or differing gifts, but shows
that when we use our talents in harmony with others we can
succeed: alone, we may not.

Why does the Bible lay such a strong emphasis on working
together? The reason is that people grow through relationships. We knock the corners off one another. We were
designed to cooperate, not to be rugged individualists. Again
the wisdom literature sums this up well.

> As iron sharpens iron, so one man sharpens another.
>
> *Proverbs 27:17*

We often interpret promises and commands of scripture individually, when they were intended to apply to the church
corporately, in line with the culture of Bible times.

## An uphill struggle

We all have difficulty keeping the first commandment – to
love God. We often have even more difficulty handling Jesus'
second commandment – to love others. We often don't like
our neighbour, colleague or fellow church member, let alone
love him. Even when we feel it might be possible, and we
want to try, we're not successful. We struggle to accept the
faults of others and they struggle to accept ours. For most
Christians, being really loving is an uphill struggle.

When we can't resolve our relationship problems, we feel
guilty. Doesn't the Bible say that love is the mark of our
discipleship? No wonder we feel wretched when relationships

with other Christians are damaged or broken. We feel failures if we don't show love.

Many non-Christians feel no such compulsion. If someone annoys them, they feel freer to avoid or reject that person or even to fight back. As Christians we acknowledge the constraints of Jesus' teaching, accepting such responses are wrong. As we shall see, even in the secular world such responses are being recognised as unproductive.

## What can we do?

We all have problems with relationships at times, but what can we do about this? Are there any solutions? If you want to, or have to, work as part of a team, there are some steps you can take to minimise the difficulties and maximise the benefits: we call this teambuilding. As marriage enrichment courses can strengthen marriages and help prevent future problems, so teambuilding can help teams to function better and weather the inevitable storms.

# A MODEL FOR TEAMBUILDING

We approach teamwork by drawing on our experience in four different disciplines, giving four different perspectives.

The first perspective is from Rosemary's counselling experience, to help you consider how you relate to others. What are you bringing into the team in terms of your attitudes and values? What do you expect from yourself, from others, from the group? Why do you react as you do?

The second perspective is from our career guidance background, to help you identify your own unique personality, gifts and abilities, and consider how you can use this knowledge to improve your teamwork. If you know and understand yourself and your gifts, and understand others and their gifts, you are better equipped to work at fitting in together. Then you can complement each other's skills and compensate for one another's weaknesses.

The third perspective is from Gordon's experience of

working in management. Much study has been done on how people work together effectively; management trainers have been helping people to improve their teamwork for many years, and have shown that team problems can be alleviated by setting goals, and having clear roles and regular reviews.

The fourth perspective is from our training and experience as Christian workers. The spiritual undergirds the other three. As Christians, it is fundamental to our approach to teamwork. What does God have to say about our relationships?

These four perspectives produce the elements that comprise our teambuilding 'model' which we believe should help you in teamwork. They are presented in four sections:

## SECTION 1: INTRODUCTION TO TEAMWORK

### Living and working with others *Chapter 2*

What is a team? . . . teams versus groups . . . teamwork pays dividends . . . teambuilding.

### What is a good team? *Chapter 3*

How do we know if our team is functioning well? . . . signs of a good team . . . symptoms of bad teams . . . different types of team.

## SECTION 2: INTERPERSONAL ASPECTS OF TEAMWORK

### Expectations and assumptions *Chapter 4*

My background (what I bring) . . . childhood experiences . . . stored wraths of the past . . . family experiences and expectations . . . cultural and denominational differences . . . values . . . personality differences . . . expectations of teamwork . . . family genograms.

## Commitment *Chapter 5*

What does team commitment mean? . . . appropriate commitment . . . David and Jonathan . . . the cost . . . unequal commitment . . . motivation and personality . . . stress.

## Communication *Chapter 6*

Communication with God . . . good listening . . . verbal versus nonverbal communication . . . feedback . . . bridge building . . . taking risks . . . confrontation . . . speaking the truth in love . . . self-image.

## Conflict *Chapter 7*

Conflict is inevitable . . . a family rift – Joseph . . . conflict styles . . . finding your style . . . dealing with hurt . . . forgiveness . . . how to resolve conflict.

# SECTION 3: INDIVIDUAL ASPECTS OF TEAMWORK

## Personality type *Chapter 8*

Understanding people . . . personality types . . . Myers Briggs Type Indicator . . . we need each other . . . problem solving as a team . . . different ways of communicating . . . different working environments . . . different lifestyles.

## Gifts and abilities *Chapter 9*

We all have gifts . . . finding our gifts . . . using our gifts in the team . . . complementing not competing . . . link between energy and gifts . . . God's rules for using our gifts . . . recognising others' gifts.

## Team roles *Chapter 10*

Roles in the early church ... teamwork research ... identifying roles ... team leader role ... successful teams.

# SECTION 4: OTHER ASPECTS OF TEAMWORK

## The team leader *Chapter 11*

Biblical qualifications for leadership ... Jesus our example ... warning to leaders ... followers ... styles of leadership ... gifts for leadership.

## Team management *Chapter 12*

Clear authority structure ... task definition ... flexibility ... managing change ... appraisal and review ... Moses.

## Growth and development *Chapter 13*

Good teams are effective ... personal growth ... teamwork develops interpersonal skills ... leadership team model ... stages of team development ... moving on.

## Spiritual perspectives *Chapter 14*

The relationship verses ... spiritual warfare ... New Testament quarrels ... forgiveness ... encouragement ... building a spiritual life together.

And finally in Chapter 15 we show you how to BUILD YOUR TEAM PROFILE.

# HOW TO USE THIS BOOK AND TEAMBUILDING MODEL

One possible way to use *Teamwork* is for every member of the team to read each chapter in turn for discussion at a team meeting. Alternatively, you may decide to set aside a weekend to work together on the book and teambuilding. Either could be a very effective use of time.

It's best to do teambuilding when the team members are engaged together in actual projects, not as a theoretical exercise before they, as a team, have begun to meet real problems. As we explain later, some of the exercises can be used as the basis of an annual team review. Of course, there may be reasons why you are unable to work together on this material, but if you do only the individual exercises, your teamwork will still improve.

## ACTIVITIES

To benefit fully from this book, you'll find it helpful, as you read through, to note anything that you feel will particularly help you and/or your team. Each chapter from now on has activities and exercises for you to do. You could record the results in your notebook. If you wish to build a profile of your team, as explained in Chapter 15, you can use these notes to do that.

## FURTHER READING AND RESOURCES

There is a list of further reading and resources on page 156.

# SECTION 1: INTRODUCTION TO TEAMWORK

## Living and working with others *Chapter 2*

What is a team?
... teams versus groups
   ... teamwork pays dividends
      ... teambuilding.

## What is a good team? *Chapter 3*

How do we know if our team is functioning well?
... signs of a good team
   ... symptoms of a bad team
      ... different types of team.

# 2

# Living and working
# with others

Getting on with other people is hard. Really cooperating and working together successfully is even harder. Yet almost all of us have to do so – at work and at home, in commerce and in industry, as well as in marriage and in the family. We are often in teams in our leisure activities as well – on the playing field, in our social life and in the church. Teams are found in all areas of life. The team model set out in this book should help in all types of teamwork, from living in a family to being part of an international outreach team; from sharing a flat to being a member of a church leadership team.

A team can be defined as 'a group of people who share common objectives and who need to work together to achieve them'. This definition surely applies to numerous aspects of Christian living. Why then do many of us find so much difficulty in working together? Why is so much effort lost through our pulling in different directions? This may be a good time to consider how committed you are to improving the way you work together. How much effectiveness is lost through poor teamwork? What priority do you give to ensuring that your team functions well? In fact, is it truly a team?

## Not all groups are teams

A team may consist of as few as two people, or as many as can reasonably work together. Once a team gets into double numbers, it may need splitting into smaller units (sports teams excepted!). The word 'team' is often used loosely. The entire workforce of a company is often referred to as a team, but in the technical sense of the word, this is not so. A team is not just any group working together. Committees, councils and task forces are not necessarily teams – we would refer to these as working groups. Working groups are necessary and effective and many of their values and methods are the same as those of teams, but that does not make them teams. They come together to share information, perspectives and insights. They make decisions that help each individual do his or her job better. But they differ from teams in that their focus may still be on individual goals and accountabilities.

The essence of a team is common commitment to a mutually agreed goal for which it holds itself responsible. There is a synergy of ideas and effort between the members that enables the team to achieve its goal far more effectively than would be possible by putting together the members' individual efforts. The team usually has leadership that brings out the best in it. It works together on tasks. Much that is written in this book will help you relate to others generally, whether in working groups or in teams. However, you need to be aware that you should not expect a working group of which you are a member to perform and behave as if it were a team.

## Teamwork in the secular world

The secular world is convinced about the value of teamwork. God designed us to function in teams, and the world has discovered that teamwork succeeds! It gets the job done. That's good in itself because most of us like to succeed. It's nice to be 'on the winning side'.

Hanging in the reception area of the Nissan car plant in Sunderland is this framed statement of company philosophy:[1]

> *We believe in teamwork, wherein we encourage and value the contribution of all individuals who are working together towards a common objective and who continuously seek to improve every aspect of our business.*

Nissan use teamwork because they have found it works. Statistics for car production in the 1980s[2] are shown below.

| | Japan | United States | Europe |
|---|---|---|---|
| Productivity (hours per car) | 16.8 | 25.1 | 36.2 |
| Quality (defects per 100 cars) | 60 | 82 | 97 |
| % workforce in teams | 69.3 | 17.3 | 0.6 |
| Suggestions per employee per year | 61.6 | 0.4 | 0.4 |
| Training of new workers (hours) | 380 | 46 | 173 |

Teamwork is high on many companies' agenda today as, following the lead of the Japanese, they are realising that only by good teamwork can they make the most of their workforce. The Japanese divide the production workforce into teams. Each team cooperates in solving problems and reaching decisions by consensus. They agree on team goals. Each member depends on the others to get results, and they even learn to do each other's jobs. This has been very successful.

We in the West are beginning to emulate them. There seems to be a growing recognition that problems belong to all, and everyone needs to pull together to solve them. When contracts are lost to overseas competitors who produce goods more efficiently and cheaply, everyone suffers. Therefore, management consultants are laying a major emphasis on training in teamwork. In order to improve performance in the 1990s and to stay one step ahead of competitors, the old order of competitive individualism is being dropped.

The Rover car company, having been bought by British Aerospace, was transformed when Honda took a twenty per

cent share. Rover was able to cooperate with Honda technically, and to take on some of its management policies and
practices. The workforce was broken down into small teams.
Morale improved enormously as a result, and so, ultimately,
did production, with reliability and quality of the product
becoming key. Ironically, this helped to make the company
so successful that it was subsequently bought by the German
quality car manufacturer BMW.

## Family model

We almost all started life as part of a small team: a family. It
is well known that the quality of family life we experience
in childhood affects our adult lives and, in particular, our
relationships. The person who grew up in a happy, secure
family is able to form good relationships more easily than
the person who grew up in a family where love, acceptance
and understanding were lacking.

He or she may have a real struggle to live a well-adjusted
life. However, just as the family, when functioning well, helps
us to mature, so membership of a well-functioning team,
which can provide a secure interpersonal environment, will
help us continue to grow.

## It adds up

A good team can produce more than the sum total of its
individual members' contributions. The old proverb says
that 'two heads are better than one'. Moreover, two heads
working together are better than two heads working
independently. 'Many hands make light work' is also true,
but only if they are working well together. Otherwise, it is
more likely to be a case of 'too many cooks spoil[ing] the
broth!'

Within the Christian church we seem to be perennially
short of workers – there is always more to do than people
willing to do it. We need to make the best use of those we
have, which is why good teamwork is so important. Working
in teams has many benefits, but there is a price to pay.
Forming interdependent relationships is costly. It takes time,

effort and commitment. Is teamwork worth what we need to put into it? We believe so.

## A waste of God's resources

The Christian church wastes a lot of time and energy – and, worst of all, it loses people – because of poor teamwork. People are lost from the team, or the church, or even from the Christian faith. Many, when they become disenchanted, move to the fringe of the church and no longer take a significant part in its life. Disillusioned with the Christian 'club', they become ineffective members of it.

To give an example: if a church choir has a new leader who wishes to bring about significant changes, she should be careful to involve the choir members in this process – to help them understand the reasons for the changes and to listen to their views – so that they feel they have a say in any decisions that are made. Carelessly implementing changes or imposing them without discussion would alienate the members and might even prove a stumbling block to their faith.

Some Christians have chosen to work alone because working with others has proved too frustrating. Sometimes, where established teams are too cumbersome, too bogged down in internal warfare, or lacking in any clear vision, God uses and blesses these 'loners'. There will always be those who will work independently. However, we are convinced that this is not the way God usually intends his people to operate.

## Following in the footsteps of Jesus

Jesus set an example of how to serve the Father here on earth, and we are commanded to follow in his footsteps. He chose to use the team approach: he gathered together a team of twelve men and shared his life with them. It wasn't always easy. There were misunderstandings, disputes and squabbles. But, Jesus wanted to teach and disciple this way. At the beginning the disciples were very ordinary men: they developed into men who changed the world. Jesus left us a fine example of teamwork.

## When teambuilding is needed

A team is especially productive in certain situations – most obviously, in those requiring other people's support. Tackling a complex task which needs a variety of skills is more effectively done by a team than by an individual. When consensus is important, then the shared decision making that should come with teamwork is instrumental in bringing it about. Teamwork can also develop strengths and compensate for weaknesses.

But good teamwork doesn't just happen. We all need to work at it, and this book suggests activities that will help. Here are some things you can do now.

# INDIVIDUAL ACTIVITIES

1 Why are you reading this book? Are you thinking of starting a team; are you in an existing team that you think could function better; are you a team leader? Make some notes of the particular team issues of which you are aware. Make them from your own perspective. For example: 'I'm thinking of sharing an apartment with two friends. It could work out well, but then again, it might not. I don't want to be trapped in an arrangement that is difficult to back out of if things go badly. How should I go about making the decision? What should we discuss when we get together to consider the idea?'
2 List below the groups in which you are involved.

| Example: | Church | Youth group leadership team |
| | | Church council |
| | | Caring group |
| | Family | Immediate |
| | | Wider |
| | Work | General |
| | | Department |
| | Leisure | Football team |
| | | Amateur orchestra |

Which of these groups would you classify as a team? Would any of these teams benefit from some teambuilding? Would any of the groups be better if they were developed into a team?

## TEAM ACTIVITIES

1 Discussion topic: Would it be simpler to go it alone than to struggle with a difficult team situation? When is it justifiable to work independently?

2 Exercises 2 (Zin obelisk game, page 163) and 3 (*Trivial Pursuit* team exercise, page 167) show that teamwork pays. They can also be used as icebreakers for teams still getting to know each other or on teambuilding days.

3 If you are about to form a team involving close personal relationships, you may find the list of 'Things to talk about' (Exercise 4, page 169) helpful.

4 Let each member of the team share a brief outline of their previous experience of working in a team.

5 Discuss each of the following parameters which contrast working groups with teams. (The 'a' statements pertain to working groups and the 'b' statements pertain to teams.) How much of a team are you? Are you what you wish to be?

1a We feel our commitment is to our own areas of responsibility.

1b We feel a sense of ownership of the team and its goals.

2a Our major focus is on individual performance.

2b Our major focus is on team performance.

3a We come together to share information, perspectives and insights.

3b We come together to solve common problems and work on common tasks.

4a The leadership style is more directive than facilitative.

4b The leadership style is more facilitative than directive.

5a Most decisions are taken by the leader.

5b Most decisions are taken by the team.

6a Relationships with one another are formal/polite.

6b Relationships with one another are informal/relaxed.

# 3

# What is a good team?

Our local football team won the FA Trophy. Only good teamwork could have achieved that. When the members of a football team are playing together well, it's obvious. They score goals and win matches. It's also obvious when they're not playing well: their efforts are poorly coordinated and they may not score any goals at all.

How do you know if you are working well as a team? What indicators are there as to whether a team is a good one or a poor one? The following may help you to assess the health of your team.

## SIGNS OF GOOD TEAMWORK

### A balanced team

A good team usually has a balanced composition. People within it have complementary skills and personality types. They fulfil different roles. In giving a ministry team to a church, the Lord gives 'some to be apostles, some to be prophets, some to be evangelists, and some to be pastors and teachers' (Ephesians 4:11). These are likely to be people of very different kinds.

What about spiritual gifts? Can't God give us the gifts which are missing from our team? Of course the Lord can give anyone the gifts needed in a particular situation. We believe he usually chooses to give us spiritual gifts that are similar to the natural gifts he has bestowed. It is not unusual to find a teacher by profession who also exercises the spiritual gift of teaching. Those exercising the spiritual gift of leadership will often be those who also have the natural gift of leadership. One meaning of the word 'charis', usually translated gift, is 'graced'. The charismata, or spiritual gifts could be natural gifts/abilities that have been graced for Christian ministry.

## Creativity and vision

A good team will tend to generate ideas, and creativity will flow. There will be a lot of enthusiasm for the task in hand. The different personalities will spark one another off into new ways of thinking and acting. There will be clear vision. (This is particularly important in any kind of leadership team.)

One church leadership team felt that they needed a new vision for the way ahead. Isn't it the Lord who gives the vision for a church? Well, yes, but usually he does it through the people in leadership. This church's leadership team members were nearly all of a similar personality type – and certainly not visionary. Most of them were the solid, reliable, 'backbone-of-the-community' type. They decided they needed to appoint some people to the team who were 'ideas' types, who had flair.

## Clear objectives

A good team has a clear team goal. Having a clear goal helps to ensure that each member is working to the same agenda. Imagine a football team where half the team is playing toward one goalpost and the other half is playing toward the other! When team members are working toward different goals, inefficiency and conflict are likely to occur. For this reason company goals are often clearly displayed for the workforce to see, and individual departments may have their own goal on the office door or wall as well.

## Openness is a key issue

Members of a good team will not be afraid to tell each other the truth. In fact the Bible links 'speaking the truth in love' to spiritual maturity and growth (Ephesians 4:15). Some people will go to enormous lengths to avoid saying what they really feel. This may be because they hate confrontation, but honesty is always necessary in conflict resolution. There is almost certainly something amiss with a team whose members are afraid to be open with one another.

## A sense of belonging

Teamwork helps to meet our basic need of belonging, of being accepted as part of a group. The weekly elders' meeting can be a time we look forward to, knowing that we shall be with those who are as concerned for us as we are for them. We know that whatever the problems we face in the church, this team has a genuine desire to find solutions. We will be valued for our contribution to those solutions.

It feels good when a team is working well. It shows on the faces of the team members. When they meet together there is enthusiasm and happiness. They want to get together at other times for social events. They don't just meet to achieve team goals. They have a sense of camaraderie. Members of a good team often say how much they have appreciated being a part of it.

## Shared decision making

I (Gordon) can think of one team of which I was a member. We had a difficult decision to make. There were four of us, all heads of department, meeting with the director. We were in his office until late in the evening. As different perceptions were shared and different views exchanged, the solution to our problem emerged. It was different from anything that any of us had anticipated – and better than any of us had thought of individually. I went home tired but happy, feeling that we had found God's purpose. I felt good at having been part of a team that had worked together to find the answer.

A few years later this team had grown to about a dozen people, each of whom seemed to be concerned only to represent his or her own department and ensure that its interests were served. I felt that we didn't face problems as a team, that the meetings had become simply a time of sharing information on what each department was doing. We were no longer really sharing responsibility. We had moved from being a team to being a working group.

## Relationships with the leader

Good teamwork can be measured by the relationship between the leader and the rest of the team. Do team members feel free to go to and confide in the leader, or do they go to others? Does the leader dominate all discussion and make all the decisions? Are solutions imposed from above or do the team members help to find them? A good team has respect for and values its leader, who, in turn, respects and values the team members.

## Mistakes can be growth points

In a good team mistakes are faced together and seen as opportunities for growth, both for the individual and for the team. Problems are also faced together. An effective team will quickly shift the focus of the problem away from one team member, and recognise it as a challenge for the whole team.

## Change and growth

Good teams change and grow. When our family was young, Rosemary helped Gordon in the administrative work in which he was involved. She had her own areas of responsibility, but he was the team leader and Rosemary was the helper. As the children grew up and left home, Rosemary found she had time and energy to take a more full-time role. Our team has changed quite considerably in that we now have equal roles, and quite often switch these with one another. This does not mean to say that we are not aware of our different gifts, strengths, and weaknesses, but rather the reverse.

Within a church leadership team a similar shift may need to occur. To begin with, the team may simply act as a sounding board for the minister. He is looking for feedback on his plans and ideas. The team grows in experience and wisdom, and becomes a group that can determine church policy together. It is able to listen to the Lord and find his direction for the church.

Healthy teams encourage personal growth in each member. People learn and gain confidence. Mike Woodcock, MP, who has worked in team development for many years, writes,[1]

> 'If a team is to be effective it needs to be continually developing itself and this in part means constantly facilitating individual as well as team development.'

Good teams have built-in mechanisms for individuals to grow and for the team to grow.

## SYMPTOMS OF A POOR TEAM

Just as we can observe the signs of a good team, so we can see the symptoms of a poor team. Some of these symptoms of poor teamwork have already been inferred in our consideration of the signs of a good team. Let's consider a few more.

### Confusion and lack of vision

Poor teams often manifest confusion. Lack of clarity as to who does what is evident. The 'I thought you were going to handle that' type of comment seems to be the norm, not the exception. We have all been in meetings where, as soon as the participants get outside, several people start enquiring what was meant by certain comments, or what was decided about other things.

Perhaps you have visited a department where every question provokes a response of 'I'm not sure' or 'We'll have to ask the boss'. The attitude is 'Don't ask me, I only work here'. This is a symptom of poor teamwork manifesting itself.

## Competition

A poor team will exhibit inappropriate rivalry within itself. Some competition within the team and/or with other departments is not necessarily a bad thing; but the main focus of the team should not be to compete. A good team has constructive relations with other teams or individuals with whom it has to liaise and work.

Many years ago Gordon worked in the development department of a company engaged in casting molten metal. A new technique was being used on a trial basis. The development team was working with the production workforce, who were used to traditional methods. Those who had been working in metal casting for many years thought they had all the answers. The development team, with their technical, scientific training in casting techniques, came up with different ideas.

Relationships between the two teams deteriorated. Each derided the other for its approach. The development team were seen as theoreticians with no practical experience; they, in turn, thought the workforce did not understand the principles involved. Things were not going well.

The managing director called everyone into his office to see if the matter could be resolved. In that meeting the bad relationships became very obvious. The managing director became quite angry, and told the teams that they each had something to offer, and that they were to go away and learn to work together. This pushed them into making more of an effort to cooperate, and the new technique was eventually perfected.

## Too much similarity

A team in which everyone is too alike is a poor team. It is unbalanced and likely to have blind spots – perhaps resulting in some of its tasks being left undone. This is the danger in inviting like-minded people onto our team – a mistake that's easily made, as we all tend to be drawn towards those who are similar to us in one way or another.

## Gossip and criticism

A poor team may exhibit even worse characteristics. Gossip and criticism may be rife among the members. There may be grumbling against the leader, or against other members of the team. Moses had trouble with his team, who happened to be his brother and sister! They grumbled against his leadership, and Miriam ended up with an awful punishment (Numbers 12).

Frustration is another symptom of a poor team. Members exhibit signs of lack of fulfilment, there is little enthusiasm for the team or for the task, creativity has ceased to flow and new ideas are at a premium: stagnation has set in.

## Fortress mentality

Poor teams are defensive about receiving external help. The good team knows when to use outside help and how to evaluate that help. The ineffective team rejects offers of help through fear of the consequences or alternatively seizes all offers of help, as it has no coherent view of how to proceed.

A team needs regular reviews. These reviews are best done with outside help. A church leadership team can invite an experienced leader from another church, or someone skilled in team reviewing. It is important that opportunity for appraisal and change are part of the routine and not resorted to only when things are disastrously wrong. Good teams monitor their own progress and effectiveness or have it monitored by others.

## Fear of change

If change can only be brought about by major conflict, that too is a symptom of a poor team. The 'any other business' slot at meetings should be an opportunity for members to put radical issues on the agenda. With the team's agreement, such issues can be brought forward for discussion and incorporation where appropriate.

When circumstances change, teams need to adapt. Marriage gives us an obvious example. You may have a good marriage at a certain point in time, but if the marriage itself does not change and grow as the circumstances change, then the marriage will not function well. Marriages can fail when children leave home, or on retirement, because the 'team' does not adjust.

## Poor interaction

Meetings where few people contribute or one person dominates, are symptomatic of poor teamwork. Such meetings may simply be question and answer sessions, or they may be characterised by a superficial level of discussion. These are meetings most people dread – and to which, if at all possible, they send their apologies!

# DIFFERENT TYPES OF TEAM

Teamwork is not an exact science. A good team is, in the end, one that works and that fulfils its function. Teams, like marriages, can vary immensely, and the criteria for good and bad teams will vary somewhat according to their type.

A business management team is bound to be more concerned with objectives, future planning and achievements than is a family unit, though both need to ensure that they listen to and try to appreciate the different gifts of each member of their team. In fact, every business management team varies, having its own individual style, which will often mirror the ethos of the company within which it works. Similarly, teams in one church may differ from those in another, because of different denominational styles.

Even within the same church, teams will differ. A finance team tends to have a high proportion of members who come from a particular personality type – people who enjoy keeping accurate records and dealing with lots of data. You would not expect to have the same balance of skills on a pastoral team that was concerned with the nurture and spiritual growth of the congregation.

## A diagnostic tool

We know when a plant is healthy and strong; we can see the signs in green leaves, strong growth, abundant flowers and fruit. We also know when a plant is not healthy; we can tell by the symptoms of diseased leaves, poor growth, few flowers and little fruit. So with teams, we can tell healthy teams from unhealthy ones by looking for the signs of good teamwork and the symptoms of poor teamwork.

## SIGNS OF AN EFFECTIVE TEAM

1 Balanced composition – of skills and personality types, gifts, etc.
2 Creativity flowing.
3 Enthusiasm for the task.
4 Clear vision.
5 Mistakes viewed as opportunities for growth.
6 Problems faced together. Focus is away from the individual, towards a challenge for the whole team.
7 Good relationships exist outside the team – individually and with other teams.
8 Open communication.
9 Friendships at other times.
10 Team knows when to use outside help.
11 Team has regular reviews.

## SYMPTOMS OF A POOR TEAM

1 Everyone is too alike, which leads to blind spots.
2 Some tasks left undone.
3 Frustration and lack of fulfilment, no enthusiasm.
4 Gossip and criticism.
5 Grumbling against one another and against the leader.
6 Meetings dominated by one person.
7 A superficial level of discussion.

8 Poor relationships within the team/with the leader.
9 Confusion and lack of vision.
10 Defensiveness about receiving outside help.

## INDIVIDUAL ACTIVITIES

1 Is my team functioning well? Is there anything I can do to help it function better?
2 Would the team be open to doing some teambuilding work? Can I bring this up at the next meeting?

## TEAM ACTIVITIES

1 Discuss the signs of good teamwork and the symptoms of poor teamwork. Which of these apply to your team?
2 Use the team satisfaction questionnaire (Exercise 5, page 173) to assess each member's satisfaction with the team.
3 How can you improve your teamwork? Can you do some teambuilding together?
4 Exercises 2 (page 163) and 3 (page 167) will help your team be aware of signs of good teamwork and symptoms of poor teamwork.

This concludes Section 1: Introduction to teamwork.

# SECTION 2: INTERPERSONAL ASPECTS OF TEAMWORK

**Expectations and assumptions** *Chapter 4*
My background (what I bring)
. . . childhood experiences
   . . . stored wraths of the past
      . . . family experiences and expectations
         . . . cultural and denominational differences
            . . . values
               . . . personality differences
                  . . . expectations of teamwork
                     . . . family genograms.

**Commitment** *Chapter 5*
What does team commitment mean?
. . . appropriate commitment
   . . . David and Jonathan
      . . . the cost
         . . . unequal commitment
            . . . motivation and personality
               . . . stress.

**Communication** *Chapter 6*
Communication with God
. . . verbal versus nonverbal communication
   . . . feedback
      . . . bridge building
         . . . taking risks
            . . . confrontation
               . . . speaking the truth in love
                  . . . self-image.

**Conflict** *Chapter 7*
Conflict is inevitable
. . . a family rift – Joseph
   . . . conflict styles
      . . . finding your style
         . . . dealing with hurt
            . . . forgiveness
               . . . how to resolve conflict.

# 4

# Expectations and assumptions

You don't come into a team empty-handed. Some of the things you bring are useful, some not. Your previous experiences, be they good or bad, are part of you. You also carry with you, in the genes inherited from your parents and forebears, all that the Lord made you when he formed you in the womb. These things can be considered as the luggage you carry when you embark on the journey of forming a team.

The expectations and assumptions that help make up your value system are crucial in determining how you relate to others. Problems in marriage often result from the expectations each spouse brings from his or her family of origin. This, the first of the interpersonal aspects in our teambuilding model, can be one of the main causes of misunderstanding.

## Your childhood

The first suitcase you carry is your family background. If you come from a happy, stable family, then you bring the experience of happy family relationships. You have been accepted and affirmed. You have learnt how to relate with warmth and trust.

Unfortunately, for many, childhood has brought bad experiences, resulting in a lack of confidence in other people. Perhaps your father walked out on your mother. Can men really be trusted? Or you may have been abused as a child, possibly by a relative or family friend, and become hesitant in committing yourself to any relationship.

You know and have experienced that the Lord is utterly

trustworthy. He has saved and redeemed you by dying for you on the cross. Doesn't this resolve all your unresolved childhood problems? Not necessarily. Salvation is also a continuous process. We all need God's ongoing salvation from day to day, until he brings us into conformity with his son. It is wonderful that you have become a Christian, but the process hasn't ended. God is still at work in you. You may be bringing some baggage which has a negative effect into future relationships.

## Stored wraths of the past

Joyce Huggett in her book on conflict[1] refers to 'stored wraths of the past' and says,

> 'You seek to relate closely with a particular person in the present. Without realising how or why, that person or situation reminds you, albeit subconsciously, of someone in your past whom you feared, or resented, or to whom you felt hostile for some reason. You stored away these wraths, maybe in childhood, maybe in adolescence, or maybe earlier in adulthood. You buried them inside you, deep down where neither you nor anyone else would see them. But they were not buried dead. No. They were buried alive, like active ingredients in nuclear waste. These dormant emotions lie in wait until a situation occurs in the present that is not unlike the past. They then set to work again with all their destructive power.'

We met two men, Mike and Harry, who had been working happily together as a team for some years. Charles was drafted in to help them. This did not work well. Charles seemed to be compatible with Harry, but not with Mike. In fact he said to him, 'You remind me of my father, and I never could get on with him.' This wasn't very helpful to Mike since he could do nothing about it.

Mary too has problems with deep roots in the past. When she was a child, her father always put her down and belittled her. He was an insecure man and rather immature, and he used her to boost his own ego. As most of us do, Mary developed her own coping mechanism. She learnt to remain quiet and keep her opinions to herself. If she said nothing, then her father could not denigrate her. Now Mary is trying to become part of a team with a group of colleagues, who have the common goal of forming a Christian fellowship group in their workplace. All the others share their thoughts on how they should go about this, but Mary keeps quiet. Actually, she has some very good ideas and feels frustrated at her difficulty in expressing them.

## Breaking free

Are we prisoners of our past? Certainly not. You can come to terms with your past even if you cannot change it. Begin by trying to evaluate the situation. Ask yourself if something about this person or situation is reminding you of the past: his or her mannerisms, tone of voice or physical appearance? Or perhaps you are simply aware that something's wrong and you cannot pinpoint it. Now ask if your reactions are appropriate to the present. Perhaps they are too powerful?

Assuming you feel that you are overreacting, it would be a good idea to seek help at this point. Explain to a Christian friend or counsellor how you were hurt in the original relationship. Ask her to pray with you about it. Tell the Lord all about the hurt you experienced. He knows about it anyway, but you will find relief by pouring it all out to him.

The next step is perhaps the hardest to take. You have to forgive the one who hurt you so much. Perhaps you feel you cannot do this. But if you do not forgive, the one you hurt is yourself. The Bible teaches that the Lord forgives us, as we forgive others (Matthew 6:14–15). He can help you to forgive, but you have to make the act of will that's required. Don't worry about feelings at this point. Just forgive as an act of will. The feelings will fall into place later.

## My family

Let's look at some luggage that I (Rosemary) bring from my family. It's not as heavy as Mary's but it is luggage nonetheless. I come from a family with three children, of whom I am the eldest. I have a younger brother and sister. This has inevitably helped to shape who I am.

The eldest child in a family is often expected to be responsible for younger siblings, and I always felt a sense of responsibility for mine. I clearly remember what happened when I was 15 years old, and my brother and I went to stay with a French family. Since I had spent a month with the same family the previous summer, I already spoke some French. Not only did I become my brother's interpreter, I was also his protector. I did his washing and ironing, and generally mothered him! I still need to guard against a tendency to rescue people, which I bring into many of my relationships.

Another piece of luggage is that I am one of the fourth generation of Christians on my father's side. My paternal grandfather was a minister, and several other relatives have been or are ministers or missionaries. Being in 'full-time' Christian service was considered by my family a very high calling, a privilege. This was a value I carried with me from childhood, and it must have coloured my expectations of how I would spend my life.

What do you bring from your family background? What are you carrying in your suitcase? You are bringing it with you into the team.

## Your culture

What about your cultural background? We (Rosemary and Gordon) are British. We can't help that nor can we change it. It is inevitably another piece of luggage we bring with us into any relationship – and, as we shared in the opening chapter, it has contributed to difficulties in relating to people of other cultures, even Americans.

Overseas Christian workers are usually called on to share not just their work, but their entire lives, within a multicultural community. Within Wycliffe the majority expatriate culture is American. In Africa we also work with African colleagues, with Europeans from many parts of Europe, and with other Britons.

Most of us who are British value our privacy, our independence and autonomy. Teamwork with others will, by its very nature, cause us to lose some of this. Other nationalities value other things. For most Americans, sociability scores pretty high and for Germans it may be efficiency. What are your cultural values and expectations? If you are joining a cross-cultural team these differences may need to be aired and mutual understanding sought.

You may think this has nothing to do with you. You may say, for instance, that you live in Britain, with a British spouse, British friends and belong to a British church. But what about subcultures within Britain? We British are not really one culture but many. What about cultural differences between northerners and southerners, working class and middle class? What about the many British whose parents or forebears are of a different ethnic origin?

Different denominations also have significantly different cultural norms. A denomination may teach that certain ways of behaving are correct, spiritual, or even the biblical pattern. In fact, they may simply be the result of that denomination's history or cultural assumptions. Such issues as the robing of the minister, the way communion is administered, and whether public prayer should be liturgical or extempore, are all examples of this.

Jesus was very aware of the cultural prejudices and wrong values of the scribes and Pharisees and spent quite a lot of time and effort trying to point these out to them. He even queried their stringent regulations regarding the Sabbath. He healed the sick, thereby working on the day of rest. He taught that 'the Sabbath was made for man, not man for the Sabbath' (Mark 2:27). The scribes and Pharisees were trying to keep the law of God they had been commanded to keep, but they had added their own cultural accretions to it. Jesus chided them: 'You have a fine way of setting aside the commands of God in order to observe your own traditions!'

(Mark 7:9). Let's hope we're not guilty of the same blindness.

## Your values

Another suitcase you carry with you is your value system. All Christians share certain values that are clearly set out in the scriptures, but there are a surprising number of values on which we differ. These are influenced by the other luggage we have been talking about. Your family of origin has inevitably helped to create your value system, as has your culture.

Certain values will be particularly important to some members of your team. Some will value equality, whereas others may prefer to work in a hierarchical team. You may value autonomy, even though you want to be part of a team.

You may wonder, 'What does the Lord think about all this? What is God's value system? What does the Bible teach us about values?' Certainly some values are absolute. We know that each individual is of supreme value to God. He created each of us and sent his son to redeem us. We know that the Lord also sets a high value on mercy and forgiveness, truth and generosity.

However, many of our values are linked to our culture. They are affected not only by our nationality, but also by our education and even by the era we live in. Some nineteenth-century missionaries used to think that it was of supreme value to get their converts clothed. Few today would hold this view. We are almost all of us equally blind to some of our own prejudices.

Our age will also affect our value system. We often refer to misunderstandings as being due to a generation gap. Younger people are usually less tied to traditional ways of doing things than older people. Older people may find it difficult to adapt to innovations.

## Your personality

You are unique. There is no-one else the same as you, there never has been, and there never will be. You bring your unique personality into the team you join. Yet, there is such a thing as personality type. Some personality types are more compatible than others. There can be personality clashes, and it is unrealistic to imagine that you will be able to get on equally well with everyone. Paul and Barnabas had such a sharp disagreement that they broke up their team and went their separate ways (Acts 15). Paul and Barnabas had very different personalities.

Differences of opinion don't necessarily have negative results. Some of the greatest Christian societies have been founded by men who went abroad under the auspices of one society, but broke away and formed another. Hudson Taylor went to China under the auspices of the Chinese Evangelisation Society but later formed the China Inland Mission. Cameron Townsend went to Guatemala under the auspices of the Bible House of Los Angeles and later joined the Central American Mission. Eventually he founded Wycliffe Bible Translators because he was frustrated at having to use Spanish Bibles rather than Bibles in the peoples' indigenous languages. Did these men break away from their societies and found others because of differences of opinion, or because they were such strong-minded individualists? Whatever the case, the Lord formed their personalities to serve his purpose, and he used events as they happened to form his church.

## Hopes and fears

We all have expectations – of how we think things will be, or even of how we think they should be. Sometimes these expectations are pessimistic, coloured by bad experiences in the past. Sometimes we experience fear and anxiety when moving into new situations: fear of the future, fear of the unknown. Perhaps others have had bad experiences in similar situations, and we have picked up their anxieties.

Sometimes however, we are over optimistic. If we have an idealistic streak in our temperament, we may approach a new team with unrealistic expectations. If we have previously been in a team that happened to be extremely successful, we may assume that a new team will be equally so.

## Being realistic

We all need hope for the future but if our expectations are too optimistic or too pessimistic, we will experience shock on encountering reality. Our adjustment to a new situation will have to be all the greater.

The idea of sharing our lives more closely with other Christians seems good, and surely it's biblical. Isn't this how God intends us to live, like the early believers who 'shared everything they had' (Acts 4:32)? In the early 1970s, many people entered Christian communities with such expectations, and many of them were disappointed. Perhaps their expectations were unrealistic.

Whatever you expect to experience in a team, you will probably have some surprises. It may help you to have thought through your expectations, your hopes and your fears and thus be able to share them with the team.

## INDIVIDUAL ACTIVITIES

1 List positive and negative aspects of each of the 'suitcases' you bring to the team, eg family, culture, values, personality.
2 See Exercise 6 (page 175) for an example of how to build your genogram (a map of your relationship experiences). Try to identify your relationship patterns using the questions listed.
3 List five words that describe characteristics that you would like to see in the team, eg openness.

Next, list five words that describe characteristics you wouldn't wish to see in the team, eg competitiveness.

## GROUP ACTIVITIES

1 Discuss what each of you brings in your suitcases:
  i Significant childhood experiences (get together in pairs to discuss your genograms – see 2 above).

ii Culture – do you all come from the same cultural background (class, ethnic origin, denomination, etc)? Discuss how this affects your team.

iii Values – each of you list five values you consider important for the team. Put them all on the whiteboard/flip chart/ohp and discuss them.

Here are some possible examples of values you might wish to include:

Acceptance and treatment of each member as a unique individual.

Trust and loyalty between us.

Expressed warmth and emotional support for one another.

Shared decision making.

Open communication.

Freedom to express feelings.

Similar doctrinal views.

Commitment to one another.

2 Expectations. Each of you write sentences beginning . . .

i I would like to see more . . . in our team.

ii I have been disappointed by . . .

iii I am concerned that we may . . .

3 Use a similarities grid (see Exercise 7 page 179) to discover areas of difference that may be worth discussing at some length.

4 Each of you suggest two characterisics of the team as it is now. If the other members agree, then write them on a whiteboard/ohp/flip chart. This will give you a picture of your team.

5 If you are just forming a team, you may find Exercise 4 (page 169) contains some useful subjects for discussion.

# 5

# Commitment –
# the essence of a team

We recently received a letter from two married couples, working together in Christian service. It said,

> 'This last one and a half years of trying to work together has been a real struggle. We are all committed to the project. By God's grace, we would like to work together in an upbuilding, supportive team. But we are all very human and could sure use some help!'

As their letter showed, they at least have the first ingredient for a successful team – commitment.

This, the second of the interpersonal aspects of teambuilding, is foundational to good teamwork. It is very difficult to help a malfunctioning team if there is little commitment. A good team doesn't just happen, it works because the members make it work.

## What does commitment mean?

Commitment involves the will. You make a decision to join the team, and to stay in the team, even if the going gets tough. One of the reasons for marriage breakdown today must be the lack of determination to solve problems and the lack of commitment to make marriage work. There is no real hope of overcoming the normal ups and downs that most relationships go through if, as soon as things get difficult, one partner says, 'That's enough, I'm off.' But it is not just marriage that needs commitment. Any successful team demands a similar act of the will on the part of its members.

This resolve is what keeps you going when things get difficult.

Commitment also involves dedication and devotion to a cause. Some companies want this kind of commitment from their senior staff team, who are expected to put company needs before personal ones. You may think this is taking things too far. Nevertheless dedication and devotion are needed if you are to achieve the goals of your team. Duty is another concept that's linked to commitment. It is a word that is not very popular these days but it must be recognised that you have a duty to be loyal, to keep your agreements and to do the best you can to help the team.

All these concepts demand a certain degree of unselfishness. You may need to put your own needs and goals on one side in order to further the well-being of the team. This is not easy, and you will need God's help.

## Appropriate commitment

Many of you are family members, with responsibility for a spouse and children or for elderly parents. Of course you need to be committed to these people. You are probably involved with your local church, with specific responsibilities perhaps for the youth work, or as the treasurer or as a house group leader. We are almost all committed to more than one group of people. You need to balance your commitments, as you cannot give exclusively to one team. Also, you cannot commit yourself to some task for the team if it means neglecting another more important task.

If asked to take on a new commitment, we find it helpful to ask what it involves. This is also a good time to explain any circumstances that may make us unable to fulfil our duties because of important previous ties. A minister friend was concerned that those taking leadership responsibilities in the church should be reliable and committed. One leader, a teacher, said he was not able to give such a high level of commitment while in the middle of exam marking. The minister felt he could live with that as long as he knew in advance.

The level of commitment you can give will change over time and therefore needs to be discussed regularly, to avoid misunderstandings. While leading the youth group, some of our local church youth leaders were still taking professional exams. It was understood that just before exam times, they would need to take some months off from leadership. If such matters are sorted out in advance, duties can be shared so that those under pressure can be relieved for a time.

## David and Jonathan

A most memorable friendship is recorded for us in the Old Testament. We are told in 1 Samuel 18 that Jonathan became 'one in spirit with David'. They made a covenant, a pledge of mutual loyalty and friendship. This commitment was to be tested in the most severe adversity when Saul, Jonathan's father, tried to kill David. Jonathan, undoubtedly struggling with divided loyalties, rescued David, thus going against his father's will. Jonathan and David's friendship and commitment endured even when it became clear that David was to replace Jonathan as the successor to his father's throne.

## Commitment is costly

All relationships are costly in terms of time and energy. When things go wrong you may be tempted to run away or withdraw from a relationship, simply to avoid the cost. It is your commitment that causes you to stay with it and work for a resolution. Similarly you may attend a church that is going through a difficult time. Maybe there are other churches nearby where you would feel more at home. Nevertheless your commitment keeps you loyal to the first church.

Commitment involves an element of denying yourself, your own desires and ambitions for the benefit of others. It is not always pleasant, but the rewards may be immense, particularly in terms of personal growth.

## Unequal commitment

Difficulties can arise when some members are more committed to the team than others. In this event there needs to be discussion, so that there is at least an understanding of why this is so. Maybe it can be resolved through negotiation.

Unequal commitment can occur in marriage. One partner may be willing to work at solving problems, even to the extent of getting outside counselling help. The other may be ready to give up and seek separation, or unwilling even to admit that a problem exists. Can one person resolve problems alone? Only to a certain extent. He must do what he can and entrust the outcome to God.

God is committed to us, even when our commitment to him wanes. It is his undying love that enables us to respond to him. 'We love because he first loved us' (1 John 4:19). We know that he accepts us and will forgive us whatever we do. This is surely a case of unequal commitment.

# MOTIVATION

A sense of duty isn't usually enough, of itself, to sustain long-term commitment. A successful team is marked by strong motivation which gives it a high degree of energy and drive. One of the tasks of the leader – we shall consider leadership more fully later – is to provide an environment in which motivation flourishes. Let's look at intrinsic motivation, that is, incentive which comes from within ourselves.

## Inner needs

We are all motivated to meet our basic inner needs or drives. One of these is the need to belong. This is a strong motivation for teamwork because as part of a team, you belong. Sometimes people express frustration in their attempts to become integrated into a church fellowship. It is not easy for newcomers to feel really involved in a large church, and we suggest that they take on a job, whether it's teaching a Sunday group, playing in the worship group, or helping to make the coffee. Having a role in a small team soon helps people feel a part of it.

Linked to our need to belong is our need for significance. We need to feel that we matter, that we are important to someone. If you are part of a team you are important to the other team members. You are needed.

We also need to feel we are doing something of value. If you belong to a team whose goals you believe are important, particularly if you feel those goals are being achieved, it will increase your motivation and commitment to the team.

## Personal preferences

While we all have the same basic physical and psychological needs and are motivated to meet these, we are, nonetheless, all different. The strength of our motivation to do different things varies according to our temperament and value system.

Some people are motivated by a task in itself – they simply enjoy doing it. This is particularly true of those who work with their hands, in arts and crafts. Artists enjoy painting a picture, musicians enjoy making music and bricklayers enjoy building a wall. Others are motivated by a challenge. They like problems to arise so that they can use their ingenuity to solve them. If there are no problems to tackle they become bored. Routine provides no motivation for them. They thrive when life is hectic. For others, routine, keeping the system going, bringing order and structure to bear, is sufficient stimulus. Too much change or disturbance of the orderly work environment is threatening and destroys their motivation. These are just a few examples of the different ways people are motivated. It is helpful to discuss motivation with the team, since what stimulates one member may lessen the motivation of another.

When Gordon was the manager of a residential Christian centre, he was responsible for leading the staff team. The challenge of developing the centre – to put up new buildings and improve the facilities – was his major motivation. Others on the team who were trying to provide basic services (maintenance, housing, catering, etc) must have been frustrated at the amount of change he introduced. No sooner had they got the system going than he would have another great idea to take them forward. What was needed was balance!

## Affirmation

Many people think that money is the major motivator for work, but this is not generally the case. People do work for reward, but that reward usually consists of many more factors than just money. When an employee is aggrieved at being underpaid, it is often because he feels he is worth more, even if he is not actually short of money. He may be thinking, 'Fred earns more than I do, yet he is not as able as I am.' He needs affirmation that he is valued.

We all need affirmation. The way it is expressed and received (more money, bigger office, warm thanks, praise when we do well) will differ for different people.

In our own work, we often do not see our boss for long periods of time. Geographical distance (most of the time we are on different continents!) means we get very little feedback. However, we do get good feedback from the people we help and this is important to us. We need feedback, just like everyone else. In Christian work this is unlikely to be in the form of a bigger pay packet or a more prestigious office. This is not what most of us are looking for anyway. We need feedback that what we are doing is worthwhile and necessary, from the minister, our boss, the team leader.

God the Father affirmed his Son, perhaps because Satan was about to sow very real human doubts about his divine mission. 'This is my Son, whom I love; with him I am well pleased' (Matthew 3:17). We get our Father's affirmation if we spend time with him. Most of us also need affirmation from those with whom we work. Appropriate feedback motivates us to work for the team goals.

## Committing time and energy

In the Old Testament, a newly married young man was not expected to go to war or have any other duty laid on him, until he had been married for a year (Deuteronomy 24:5). The year was for working on his relationship with his wife. When a couple get married in the middle of overseas service, missions often try to give them time and space to adjust to their new roles as spouses, so that they do not have too heavy a work programme at the beginning of their married life.

However, it has not always been recognised that singles also need time to work on significant relationships, and this omission can sometimes have painful results. We have many single women translation teams in Wycliffe, either working as a partnership or within a larger group of colleagues. Building these teams takes time and energy. Forming a team has not always been considered as work, and people have sometimes been expected to do this at the same time as trying to learn a new language and adjust to living in a Third World rural village. It has been assumed that they will produce large amounts of technical materials in preparation for translation work when they are struggling with relationships.

In the early months of a team's formation, we suggest that you make teambuilding a priority. The team is unlikely to gel if you do not give it the time and energy it needs.

## Stress and commitment

Relationships can give us our biggest joys; they can also cause our biggest stresses. Creating a relationship, building a team or resolving difficulties with others, will take emotional energy. You need to be aware of this. If you are involved in too many other significant (and therefore stressful) life events at the same time, they will all be drawing on your emotional reserves. You need to beware you don't 'run your tank dry'.

Relationship adjustments are a major component of many stressful life events – marriage, divorce, the death of a spouse, and so on. Even a joyful event can be stressful in that it depletes our reserves of emotional energy. When we are under pressure, our relationships suffer, particularly those that are close; we get irritable and snappy, or we withdraw into our shell. When one member of a family is under particular pressure, it can cause tension and difficulty all round. Recognising that outside pressures are affecting your relationships can bring understanding and relief as these are talked through and allowances and adjustments made.

## Recognising stress symptoms

Some of us have less capacity to tolerate stress than others. This may be because of our temperament, our state of physical health, or for many other reasons. For all of us, our tolerance of stress fluctuates.

Just as people have different levels of tolerance to stress, so we have different stressors (things that cause us to feel stressed), differing reactions to stress, and different ways of coping. For example, under pressure one person will want to get as many decisions made as soon as possible, while another will prefer to defer all decision making until she feels more relaxed. If one team member prefers one mode and the other prefers another, they can compound the stress by pressuring each other to conform to their preferred mode.

Since stress affects our ability to relate to others and our ability to fulfil our commitments, it is important that we understand our own stress behaviour and, if possible, that of other team members. Discussing this together can take us to a new level of understanding and intimacy.

## Commitment is crucial

Commitment is important in any relationship. The team whose members are not really committed to it and its goals is unlikely to succeed as a team. Commitment is the glue which holds it together. 'The essence of a team is common commitment. Without it, groups perform as individuals; with it, they become a powerful unit of collective performance.'[1]

# INDIVIDUAL ACTIVITIES

1 List all your commitments at this time. How many of them are team commitments? Are they realistic? Can you fulfil them all properly? Is there adequate time for personal needs (time with the Lord, time for family, time for self/relaxation)?
2 You may feel that some of your team activities take a lot of time but you get little satisfaction from them. Your

commitment is low and/or you are not highly motivated. What is it that motivates you?

3 Which of your commitments do you feel a duty to fulfil even if they do not give you a lot of satisfaction?

4 What other factors in your life are causing you pressure (eg midlife adjustment, examinations, redundancy, broken engagement, bereavement)?

5 Do you feel affirmed in the team? What tells you that you have done well and are appreciated? Do you affirm the others?

## TEAM ACTIVITIES

1 Discuss the level of commitment that the team expects. What other commitments do each of you have?

2 Discuss your team's motivation. Is the group motivation the same as that of each individual member, or are some of you struggling because you are motivated differently from the majority? Can you switch jobs within the team and thus become more motivated? (See Chapters 8 and 9 for development of differing roles and gifts.)

3 Each team member state one thing she enjoys about being in the team and one thing that is costly to her.

4 Explain to each other:
   i What stresses me.
   ii How you can know I am under pressure.
   iii How I would like to be treated when under pressure (eg left alone, have someone to talk to, allowed to get out and relax, helped to get the job done).

# 6

# Communication – oiling the parts

Good communication is essential for any effective team, and the most important ingredient in any relationship. If we are to succeed in friendship, flat-sharing, marriage, business teams, or working together in Christian service, we must learn to communicate openly and clearly with one another. It is of vital importance to work at this.

## Communication with God

God created man to have fellowship. Each evening, the Lord would come and walk and talk with Adam and Eve in the garden. Communication was undoubtedly full and open. There was no kind of barrier. That communication broke down when man sinned. From then on there was prevarication, subterfuge and deceit on man's side. The relationship was badly damaged, but God longed to restore it.

Throughout the Old Testament we see God seeking to communicate with his people, the Jews. He instituted the Law, he made covenants, he sent prophets. However, it was not until the Messiah came that it was possible for God's relationship with man to be restored. Jesus was his ultimate communication, the Word incarnate. Jesus came to heal the rift between God and man, and he gave his life to restore open communication.

# LISTENING

Listening is an important part of communication. Without listening well, I will never really understand what another person is saying, let alone what he or she is feeling. Unfortunately, many people respond to what they *think* another person is saying, when this is actually their own interpretation of what is being said.

## The Bible teaches effective listening

Proverbs 18:13 says, 'He who answers before listening – that is his folly and his shame.' Yet we all do this to some extent. Instead of really listening, we find ourselves formulating what we want to say while the other person is still speaking.

In Jesus we see an example of someone willing to give himself completely to others. When he met the woman at the well, he was very tired, yet he took time to discover her real need and address it. When Lazarus died and his sister, Mary, was weeping, Jesus wept with her, entering into her pain (John 11:33). This giving of ourselves to others is what real listening is all about.

1 Peter 3:8 tells us to 'be sympathetic, love as brothers, be compassionate and humble.' The Greek word translated 'sympathetic' here means entering into another's feelings and taking them on as though they were your own. This frees you from judging, condemning or disagreeing. You may disagree with another's actions or words, but you cannot disagree with her feelings. They just *are*.

## How can we be good listeners?

In James 1:19 we are told to be 'quick to listen, slow to speak'. This is not easy. Most of us are wrapped up in our own affairs, and this often prevents us from listening properly to other people. If you are trying to team with others, you need to communicate with them, and to do this you must learn to put your problems to one side and listen.

If you can enter into what someone is feeling and feel with him, it will help both of you. It's often useful to 'reflect back' in your own words what the person has just said, to ensure that you've really understood. In the Navy, where miscommunication could cost lives, all instructions are repeated back. 'Ten degrees to port.' 'Ten degrees to port it is, sir.' Careful listening also demonstrates that you accept a person even if you don't agree with what she is saying. This acceptance will help her to feel good about herself and about you.

When we are listening, our attitudes are important. If you are feeling defensive then you are apt to be closed, to filter out anything you do not want to hear. Equally, if you have an attitude of disapproval, the speaker will pick this up from your verbal or nonverbal cues (body posture, tone and volume of voice, facial expression, etc) and will only tell you what she thinks is acceptable to you. We should try to nonjudgmental, especially during strategic conversations.

## Nonverbal communication

Another person's nonverbal behaviour can tell us a great deal about what he is feeling. As part of our job, we used to debrief Christian workers on their arrival back from a term of service overseas. Sometimes it was the nonverbal communication that told us the most. Whether someone looked sad, confused, worn-out, or alert, bright-eyed, on top of life, all communicated to us how he had fared.

Silence can speak louder than words. Perhaps there are certain topics which are not mentioned. These may be the very ones that need most discussion. Maybe a subject is so painful that it is avoided. If someone suddenly changes the topic of conversation this may be a pointer that the issue under discussion was becoming too sensitive for her and she did not want it aired.

It is good to be aware of what you are communicating to another person. It is possible to miscommunicate by your actions. Carrying on writing while someone is talking to you, or simply not looking at him, may make it seem as though you are not really interested in the person or in what he has to say, even though this may not be the case. Give the speaker your full attention. Try not to interrupt – when he pauses, ask for clarification if you need it.

## Verbal communication

Communication is a two-way process. In order to communicate within your team, you have to speak as well as listen. Aim for clarity in speaking, as much as accuracy in listening. Clarity involves being precise and specific, and if you can manage to achieve this, you are less likely to be misunderstood.

How do you go about it? To communicate clearly, it helps to be brief. Rambling all over the place will not help your listener. Try to be direct as well as concise. Looking at the person you are talking to should help. Say what the specific problem is, don't generalise, and *always* avoid ambiguity.

## Giving and receiving feedback

A good way to improve your communication skills is to give and receive feedback. This can be particularly effective in the close relationships involved in teamwork. You can ask questions like, 'Is what I said clear to you?' or 'How does what I said make you feel?' In giving feedback, you can say how you are feeling. 'I'm sorry, I can't follow what you're saying' or 'I feel you're angry with me when you speak like that.'

People continuously give us feedback on how we affect them, albeit unintentionally. What we need is sensitivity to understand what they are saying and doing. What are their volume and tone of voice, body posture, etc, telling us? What are they really saying and feeling?

## The environment for communication

The environment or climate in which we attempt to communicate is very important. If there is warmth between us and if we trust and respect one another, communication on any level will be much easier. If mistrust has built up between us – or coldness, or even hostility – establishing good communication is much more difficult. If there are barriers, the risk of not hearing or not being heard is much greater. Where there are lots of unresolved issues, communication is clouded by old disagreements, conflicts and hurts. New disagreements are seen in the light of these old hurts. Unresolved issues need to be resolved so that a trusting environment can be built.

One minister meets the two elders of his church every week to discuss business. They have created such an environment of trust between them that they can dare to be truthful. When one of them gets his toes trodden on, he feels free to say, 'I was put out to discover that you allowed the vestry to be used on Wednesday, when we had agreed all use of that room was to be referred to me.' Apology and forgiveness can take place and relationships are kept sweet.

## Bridge builders and blasters

Try to build an environment of trust in the team. Bridge building can help. Bridges are built by encouraging and affirming others and by giving appropriate praise. Acts of kindness let people know you care. Taking the time to enquire how they are, about their family, etc, all help to build a relationship, aid communication and avoid misunderstanding.

Avoid bridge blasters, such as making judgments, being critical and using harsh words. If you cause a breach, it can take years to rebuild the relationship. If people trust you then they give you the benefit of the doubt when you communicate badly. If there is no trust then they are more likely to jump to the wrong conclusions. We tolerate behaviour in a person we like which we would not accept from someone else.

Openness helps create a climate of trust. Genuineness, honesty, respect and a real concern for people's well-being, considering others more than ourselves, all build this climate of trust. Building bridges is not simply an exercise to get what we want. It is living with biblical attitudes and actions. Read the 'Relationship verses' again (Exercise 1, p 160); you will see that building bridges is simply living God's way.

# CONFRONTATION

## Taking risks

Sometimes it is necessary to take risks in order to improve a relationship. This may involve being more assertive than usual. If you don't say what you want, how can anyone else know what your needs are? An even bigger risk is confrontation. Some people find this harder than others. I (Rosemary) find it very hard to confront anyone. However, I am learning that, used carefully and appropriately, confrontation can lead to better communication. One particular relationship started badly through various misunderstandings. Attempts to resolve this by letter just seemed to make things worse. Eventually the opportunity came for a face-to-face meeting. I decided it was also the opportunity for confrontation, which thankfully led to understanding and resolution. The relationship, based on openness, is now on a much firmer footing.

## Avoidance

Most of us avoid confronting others when we feel their actions or words are wrong. The last person to know of their shortcomings is often the person concerned. The secular world seems better at confronting than the Christian world. Many modern companies have regular feedback and appraisal, giving opportunity for discussion of possible weaknesses as well as affirmation of strengths. Our observation is that Christians are loath to do this. In churches and Christian organisations we avoid discussing perceived shortcomings and fail to confront behaviour that needs confronting, possibly because we are dealing with voluntary workers who give their time freely, or because we want to exhibit love and kindness.

## Confrontation in teams

We have worked with teams in which there is little or no confrontation. The members are polite to each other, but this doesn't necessarily mean that they are working together well. Those in one team simply disliked disagreement or confrontation: maintaining harmony was important to them. We tried to persuade them to feel free to say what they thought and even to disagree, so that they had the benefit of different points of view. A team that has disagreements and occasionally even sharp words is not necessarily a bad team. It may be that it is open and honest, that people are saying what they think and feel. This is good communication.

## Truth and love

One phrase that we often encounter when working with teams is, 'I never knew you felt like that, you never said so.' In Ephesians 4:15, Paul tells us to speak the truth in love. We Christians often stress the love and fail to speak the truth. We so want to appear loving that we hide what we really feel and feed back to others what we think they would rather hear. Both truth and love are needed if we are to avoid misunderstanding. By confronting one another, by speaking the truth in love, we can avoid conflict and pain later.

What happens when we fail to confront? Often we still indicate – by nonverbal means – our unease, disapproval, or downright opposition. But since we are not specific, refusing to tell someone clearly just what we disagree with and why, the other person merely senses that things are not right. This can lead to more misunderstanding than if we had confronted the situation clearly in the first place. The very thing we have tried to avoid we precipitate in an unhelpful way.

We have a responsibility to communicate to others how we feel and what we think. If we fail to do so we are being dishonest – we are letting them down. This is particularly important for the members of a team, who should have a high degree of commitment to each other.

We find that our Dutch colleagues tend to speak their

minds clearly and this directness can be disconcerting to both Britons and Americans. However, we have seen that it brings out into the open problems that otherwise might have festered under the surface, leaving team members frustrated and unhappy. Once problems are brought out, they can be discussed and resolved.

## A high team value

Openness and honesty almost always score high in a team's value system. Most team members usually want others to be frank with them, and not to hide their feelings. We all need to practise openness but it is particularly important in teamwork. Confronting others, being open with them about how we feel and what we think, will lead to growth in us, growth in others, growth in our relationships and growth in the effectiveness of the team. It is a way to maturity.

A team of Sunday group teachers meets each month to plan and pray together. Simon feels that his class is disrupted far too much by Sandra's class, which meets in the next room and is very noisy. At the monthly meeting, he tries to refer to this problem obliquely, by suggesting that the partitioning is too thin. What does this achieve? Not a lot. It has wasted discussion time, and Sandra still hasn't realised what the problem really is.

How could Simon tackle this situation better? He could go to Sandra alone and discuss the subject with her. This is risky and he needs to be careful not to be critical or judgmental. If the discussion goes well, he will have achieved what he wanted and her class will be quieter. Maybe he will have been able to help her with some of her difficulties in controlling the class. Probably their relationship will be closer.

## Levels of communication

Communication takes place on different levels. Much of our everyday conversation goes on at a cerebral or 'head' level. It concerns facts, ideas, thoughts, advice, solutions and judgments. In close personal relationships, it's good to work at taking communication to 'heart' level, at least some of the time. When we communicate at heart level, we talk about feelings and attitudes, we disclose our true self. We are able to show empathy, understanding and affection.

Building intimacy in this way is extremely important in marriage; it is important in other close relationships too. It involves taking risks, for you may be misunderstood. You may wonder if other people can really understand how you're feeling. They are certainly more likely to understand if you try to tell them! Equally, the only way you will really be able to understand other people is to practise empathy, that is, putting yourself in their shoes. Developing this kind of intimacy involves sensitivity. When you are sensitive to another person's feelings, it frees her to be open with you in return. It is possible to learn to be sensitive. For example, a change in someone's behaviour towards you may indicate that something has gone amiss in your relationship. Perhaps he is only speaking to you on a head level. You can ask yourself why. Have you somehow caused offence? It may be necessary to ask him that, and be prepared to make amends.

## Self-image

An indispensable element in your communication is *you*. How do you see yourself? In order to communicate well with others, you need a good self-image. You need to be self-aware and at ease with yourself. Poor self-esteem will make you feel you are not worth communicating with, or hypersensitive, so you imagine slights that do not exist. You will expect to be rejected; consequently this prophecy is likely to be fulfilled.

What can you do about poor self-esteem? Your insecurities can be a major stumbling block to good relationships and effective teamwork. We addressed this problem in our book on gifts, *Naturally Gifted*[1]; in it there is a self-esteem inventory. Simply recognising that your reactions stem from low self-esteem can help you to modify them. Talking things through with a sympathetic friend or counsellor may also help. One useful exercise is to consider how the Lord views you. You can do this by meditating on the Bible passages that teach us how much he loves and values us.

## Communication and teambuilding

Communication is one of the key building blocks of an effective team. Individuals need to feel accepted, understood, supported, respected and involved if they are to contribute well to the team. All these things require good communication.

Where there is poor communication you will probably have a poor team. There may be frustration, misunderstanding, grumbling, poor cooperation and a lot of wasted energy. In fact the task may never be achieved, because so much energy is dissipated on other issues.

# INDIVIDUAL ACTIVITIES

**1** Rate yourself out of five on each of the following aspects of good communication:

| | |
|---|---|
| Listening | ____ |
| Empathising | ____ |
| Unambiguous speech/writing | ____ |
| Reading nonverbal behaviour in others | ____ |
| Giving feedback | ____ |
| Building a trusting environment | ____ |
| Taking risks/being vulnerable | ____ |
| Good self-esteem/lack of defensiveness | ____ |
| Keeping an open mind/not judging | ____ |
| Able to confront | ____ |
| **Total** | _____ |

If you score over 40 you probably have good communication skills. If you score under 20 you are in need of help in communicating with others.

**2** Which aspects of communication are you weak on? Try to develop a strategy to improve these. A good friend may be able to help you.

**3** How well do you handle different confrontation situations?

Rate yourself in the following situations, using a scale of 1 to 10:

As confronter  As confrontee

   i With your parents
  ii With your spouse
 iii With close friends
 iv With fellow workers
  v With those in authority
    over you
 vi With those you have
    authority over
 vii With your children
viii With men in general
 ix With women in general

Average the scores that apply to you. If you average 7 or above, you confront well. If you average 4 to 6, consider the situations on which you score low and try to see why. If you score 3 or less then you need help with confrontation.

Adapted from work by Dr Ken Williams of Wycliffe Bible Translators.

## TEAM ACTIVITIES

1 Discuss the results of individual activity 1. Do other team members agree with your own assessment?

2 Role plays. In pairs, act out the following, taking it in turns to play each role. The rest of the team can observe and comment. Use the communication helps suggested in the text.

   a) Your flatmate is a messy housekeeper even to the point of being insanitary. Take the initiative and talk it over with him.

   b) Your mission colleague, who is not very outgoing, spends most of her time at her desk, and little time talking to the local people. Talk to her about your feeling that she needs to get to know the people more if she is ever going to evangelise them.

c) You've heard at second-hand that a member of your youth leaders' team is thinking of giving the team up. You've sensed he's not happy. Talk to him about it.

3 Discuss whether you give sufficient time to communication in the team. Do you keep each other adequately informed? Would more frequent meetings be a good use of time? Does each one feel he or she is heard?

4 In pairs, one person tells the other a fairly complicated incident from her own life for three minutes, going into as much detail as possible. The listener then retells the story and the other person should be able to judge how much she communicated and he listened. Reverse the process.

5 In pairs, tell an incident from your life that you feel sad about. The first time you tell it your partner should give you no verbal feedback, and their nonverbal behaviour should indicate lack of interest. Tell the same incident a second time, with your partner giving good verbal and nonverbal feedback to show that he wants to hear what you have to say.

Then reverse the roles, so that he speaks and you listen to his story both ways. Discuss how it felt in each case.

6 'Speaking the truth in love, we will ... grow up into ... Christ' (Ephesians 4:15). Does your team have the balance right? Are you honest with one another? Perhaps you speak the truth too freely and neglect to temper it with love. Discuss how this balance is handled in your team.

7 Here is a feedback model you could use or adapt. Be aware that some might find it threatening, particularly in a new team where intimacy and trust have not yet developed.

Feedback from _____ to _____

   i The things I most value about you are ...
  ii Your major strengths are ...
 iii Your most helpful actions in this team have been ...
 iv I see your weaknesses as ...
  v The types of behaviour I would like to see you change are ...

# 7

# Conflict is inevitable

Conflict is inevitable in teamwork. Two people in a close relationship are bound to have disagreements. Where more than two are involved, there are even more possible combinations and permutations. It is important that we grapple with conflict, the last of the interpersonal aspects of teambuilding. How this is expressed and, more importantly, resolved, will depend to a large extent on the quality of communication. Communication and conflict resolution go together.

Conflict need not always be bad for us, for it is normal and natural; yet we fear it and often try to avoid it. What is important is not absence of conflict, but how we handle disagreement when it arises.

When we (Gordon and Rosemary) first started going out together and building a relationship, there were some arguments and disagreements. We used to try to phone each other every evening if we couldn't meet, and these calls sometimes ended with the phone being put down abruptly! We had two other friends who started going out together at the same time. They never appeared to argue, and sometimes they would tell us to stop bickering. Our own relationship deepened as we learned to understand each other and as we negotiated our way through the problems that arose. We have been married for over thirty years (we still bicker at times). The other couple never developed beyond a teenage friendship.

## It doesn't feel good at the time

When a relationship breaks down, we feel vulnerable and want to hide. That happened to Adam after he had broken God's command:

> But the Lord God called to the man, 'Where are you?' He answered, 'I heard you in the garden, and I was afraid because I was naked; so I hid.'
>
> *Genesis 3:9,10*

God took the initiative and went looking for Adam after Adam's sin had broken the relationship between them. Adam had literally tried to hide from God – an impossible task!

Sometimes people do hide away physically simply to avoid meeting another person. It is also possible to hide emotionally, and reduce a relationship to a lesser level of intimacy, which feels like coldness to the other person. We have all heard it said, 'We used to be quite close but I can't get close to him now.' We all dislike facing up to unpleasant situations or confronting people. Confrontation involves acknowledging there is a a problem and seeking to address it. We would prefer to pretend the problem does not exist.

What do you do when you've wronged others, or when others wrong you? Usually a breach in a relationship comes about because both parties have made mistakes. How do you set about restoring the broken relationship? Often we hope that, if we do nothing, the situation will revert to its previous better state. We think 'It's best to say nothing. It will soon blow over.' But unresolved issues tend to damage mutual trust, and it's far better to deal with problems as soon as possible. Unfinished business has a way of cropping up again until it is finally dealt with.

## A family rift

Joseph's brothers sold him into slavery. Years later, when he was the governor of Egypt, they were brought before him. When Joseph revealed to them who he was, 'his brothers were not able to answer him, because they were terrified at his presence' (Genesis 45:3).

Joseph understood that part of the problem was that they felt guilty and were angry with themselves. He did not deny their wrongdoing or pretend it had not happened. Rather, he tried to show them that God had worked things out for good: 'Do not be angry with yourselves for selling me here, because it was to save lives that God sent me ahead of you' (v5). This openness on Joseph's part opened the door to reconciliation. We read 'he kissed all his brothers and wept over them. Afterwards his brothers talked with him' (v 15). Communication was restored because Joseph did not deny the problem but faced it realistically. He did not attack his brothers or condemn them. He forgave them. He recognised God's sovereignty in the events of his life. This meant the past could be discussed and resolved.

We said in the last chapter that Rosemary dislikes any sort of confrontation and seeks to avoid it. This is not always wise. As we've seen in the cases of both Adam and Joseph, when one party confronts another it can often bring resolution. Gordon, on the other hand, tends to confront others more easily, sometimes when it would be best to let the matter drop. It's a matter of how and when to do it appropriately.

## How do you react to conflict?

Since we are all sure to disagree at times, we should learn to disagree effectively! We need to understand ways of resolving conflict. We each have our own preferred conflict style, or combination of styles, the one(s) that we are more likely to use than others. Each style can be valid depending on the situation. Here are some situations where various conflict styles may be appropriately or inappropriately used.

1 **Win** . . . 'I must win or all is lost.' This can be appropriate in emergencies when quick action is essential, or on important issues where unpopular decisions have to be made.

A group of aid workers was in a developing country which was plunged into civil war. They met to discuss the situation. Most wanted to stay but the director decided everyone must leave the country. It was not a popular decision, but he believed it was necessary for safety's sake. This was a situation requiring a fast decision, and he felt it was important enough for him to overrule the others.

An inappropriate use of this conflict style would be by those who have to win all the time. Such people can be described as argumentative, as needing to control. They can be difficult to live with and should learn to use other styles of handling conflict.

**2 Withdraw** ... 'I can't win, or it's too painful to continue the dispute, or continued opposition would damage my cause irrevocably, so I withdraw.' This approach can give time for both parties to cool down. It may be appropriate when the issue is peripheral to a more major one. Withdrawing simply leaves the conflict as it is. It says, 'I don't agree but I am not going to do anything about it.'

Heather and Jim have been married just a few months. They are still working at constructive ways to resolve the inevitable conflicts that arise between them. One day they have a big disagreement. Heather gets very upset and cries a lot. Jim suggests that they put the issue to one side, and 'make up'. This is quite a struggle for Jim to do, because he is by nature a competitor with a tendency to try to win. Later, when Heather is calmer, they can discuss the disagreement more objectively and come to a resolution with which both are happy. This is a good use of withdrawal in order to resolve things later.

An inappropriate use of withdrawal is to become silent and to stop interacting with others for fear of conflict. We know of one marriage in which, when conflict looms, the wife runs away, and the husband does not know where she has gone, nor (often) why she has gone.

**3 Yield** ... 'I give in to keep the peace or when the issue is too trivial to pursue, or when I see I am wrong.' This may seem similar to withdrawing, but leads to a different result – the ending of the conflict by one giving in.

Inappropriate yielding occurs when someone gives in continually to other people and therefore does not have his own needs met. A team of two in which one is always a 'yielder' is not building a good basis for a long-lasting partnership, especially if the other person is always a 'winner'. It may work for a short time. Eventually, however, the 'yielder' will stop yielding and his built-up frustrations and resentments will emerge in an outburst of anger.

Andrew is a member of St Luke's church council. He feels strongly that St Luke's should be more involved in the local community, and specifically in helping the rescue home for alcoholics and drug addicts. When he brings this up at a meeting, he realises that most of the other members feel that the church is already overstretched. At first he argues his case, but then senses that this is causing the opposition to harden against him. His best ploy is to yield. To continue to argue would damage relationships and he probably wouldn't win anyway.

4 Compromise . . . 'I give a little, the other person gives a little – each wins a little.' This can be used appropriately when two parties have separate goals (eg in wage negotiations). It can also be appropriately used when a quick solution is needed because time is short.

Mark and Sarah are running the Christian Union at college together. Their ideas of how this should be done are very different. Mark is all for concentrating on evangelism. Sarah thinks they should give priority to building up the Christians in the group through Bible study and fellowship. They come to an agreement to give some attention to both – a good compromise. This method falls down if neither party feels satisfied with the outcome, if both consistently feel that they are only partially achieving their objectives.

5 Resolve . . . both sides win if differences are resolved. It is appropriate to use resolution when both sets of concerns are too important to compromise. It can be used to gain commitment to the final decision by all parties concerned, or to merge insights from people with different perspectives.

With important issues, this style is probably the best one to use. In Christian marriage, it is certainly the one to strive for, even if another method is used first, as in the example of Jim and Heather above. Similarly, with teamwork, it's worth trying to work towards resolution if possible. It takes time and energy, but if resolution is achieved, everyone feels satisfied. Some people think that this method of conflict resolution is the best one or the only one that should be used. We feel there are appropriate times to win, yield, compromise or withdraw, as well as to resolve.

It is important to know how to resolve conflict, and we will talk more about this later. But first, let's consider your conflict style.

## Your conflict style

It may help the team if you recognise and discuss your usual way of handling conflict. One member may try to win all disagreements, using the 'win' style, sometimes inappropriately. Another may yield in all circumstances. This latter person may actually have good ideas, and the team may be losing some needed input because the 'yielder' has not learned how to confront appropriately.

Gordon knows that if Rosemary goes very quiet (withdraws) then he had better try to find out what is wrong. Rosemary knows that if Gordon becomes more persuasive, increasing arguments to justify his position (to win), she had better get to the bottom of what is troubling him.

A team where compromise is exclusively used will never be able to implement a difficult policy fully. Half-heartedly introducing such a policy to keep everyone happy is usually ineffective. Time and effort need to be expended to bring about resolution.

Half the youth team want to arrange a sunshine holiday abroad for the youth group. The others would rather go on a walking holiday in Scotland. They compromise and take a holiday in Cornwall where there are some beaches and some walking. It rains and so the young people do not get much of a beach holiday and the clifftop walks are a poor substitute for the grandeur of the Scottish mountains. It would have been better to have worked for resolution rather than settle for this compromise. Perhaps they could have gone to the Mediterranean one year and Scotland the next.

Let us recognise and understand our own and others' conflict styles. Let's try to broaden our use of all the five styles.

Let's learn to confront disagreements and resolve problems using an appropriate conflict style.

# HOW TO RESOLVE CONFLICT

## Acknowledging the problem

Whenever conflict exists, you have to confront the situation. That is, you must recognise that you have a problem. Then you can think through the best way to handle it. If there is another person involved and you decide that it would be best to avoid tackling that person openly (as it sometimes will be), you will still have confronted the problem. That is the most important thing. The problem won't go away, and if it is not dealt with it could become worse – even unresolvable.

## Mind your language

Resolution involves talking, and words have power. 'The tongue also is a fire, a world of evil among the parts of the body' (James 3:6). It is helpful to be aware of how certain ways of expressing differences of opinion can make disagreements worse while other ways can help to resolve them. 'Reckless words pierce like a sword,' says Proverbs 12:18, 'but the tongue of the wise brings healing.'

Avoid attacking your opponent, especially his character. Try to state clearly how you feel, rather than blaming the other person. Use 'I' messages to do this. For example, you could say, 'I was disappointed when you didn't come to pick me up for the house group meeting', rather than, 'You're so disorganised. If you kept a diary you wouldn't have forgotten me the other night.' Some words are best avoided. These include 'always' and 'never'. If someone says to you, 'You always do this', you feel under attack. It's not true, anyway. None of us are that consistent. 'Never' is much the same.

John usually comes in from work, goes upstairs to get changed into his jeans, and leaves his suit thrown on the bed. This annoys Judith, his wife. 'You never hang up your suit,' she says to him, as part of their quarrel about his untidiness.

Actually he does sometimes. She might find it more productive to say, 'I seem to have a lot of clearing up to do after the children. I feel myself getting annoyed when I find your clothes have not been put away either.'

Keep to the issue and don't drag up other grievances. In the midst of a disagreement, some people bring in so many other factors that it is almost impossible to tell the wood from the trees. When Helen came to the team meeting, she wanted to discuss timing of the meetings. As a mother of small children, her time was at a premium. Unfortunately she had some strong feelings about being undervalued by the team and clouded the issue by bringing these in too. She left the meeting without resolving the issue of meeting times.

## When feelings are hurting

Often in disagreements we threaten or hurt the other person. In such cases you need to deal with the hurt before you can move on to solving the problem. Probably both of you are hurting. This is the time for open discussion of your feelings and for listening carefully and trying to understand each other. Apologies are probably needed on both sides.

## Forgiveness

Secular literature on teamwork recognises that conflict issues need to be faced and resolved. It does not often mention forgiveness. This is not to say that secular sources do not recognise that harbouring resentment and holding bitterness are destructive. They do. However for Christians, forgiveness is mandatory. It is at the heart of the Christian message. God will not forgive me if I have not forgiven those who have wronged me. This is illustrated very plainly in the parable Jesus told of the unmerciful servant (Matthew 18:21–35).

In teamwork you will get hurt and you will be offended. As Christians we have to forgive. This means we forgive any wrongs we receive by a conscious act of will. It's nothing to do with the way you feel. It's something that you decide you will do. In answer to Peter's question about how often we should forgive others, Jesus replied, 'seventy-seven times'

(Matthew 18:22). That's a lot of times.

## Barriers to reconciliation

If you have noticed there's a problem in the team – maybe a difference of opinion over a specific issue, or you feel you're not pulling well together and there are unresolved tensions – what can you do about it? Maybe the others don't see there is a problem or are not really committed to working as a team. If even one member of a team doesn't want to resolve differences, it makes finding a solution much more difficult.

It may help to discuss what is involved in being a team. We are back to the basic issue of commitment. Sometimes when we're working with a married couple over a particular conflict, we ask them quite bluntly, 'Do you want this marriage to work?' Resolving conflict takes time and energy. It is only worth doing if commitment is there. So, if you want to resolve a conflict with someone who does not appear to want to work at it, what you do may depend partly on how important the issues are to you. Should you yield? Can you compromise? Sometimes it helps if an outsider is brought in as peacemaker – although even this is difficult if one party is intractable or denies that a problem exists.

## Mediators

There are many examples in the Bible of someone acting as a mediator between contending parties.

> 'I plead with Euodia and I plead with Syntyche to agree with each other in the Lord. Yes, and I ask you, loyal yokefellow, help these women . . .'
>
> *Philippians 4:2,3*

Paul is asking the yokefellow to act in this capacity. Joab mediated between David and Absalom (2 Samuel 14:1–23) and Jesus himself is the mediator between God and men (1 Timothy 2:5).

The Quakers are the only denomination that takes mediation seriously. Probably many people in other denominations could also benefit from it. Perhaps the reason mediation help is not often sought is because of a reluctance to admit that there is conflict. If we pretend conflict doesn't exist we are unlikely to look for – or to find – solutions to it. It is surprising how often long-standing conflicts can be resolved with outside help.

Pauline Bell and Pauline Jordan[1] say that the benefits of mediation are that it offers both sides a procedure which:

'* values their emotions
* provides an active listener or audience through the mediator
* brings the parties together in a safe place
* empowers people so that they can choose how much or how little to say
* explores perceptions in order to focus the issues
* restores proportion and perspective
* builds on common ground
* uses a process so that people can defend their interests without overwhelming the other party.'

The mediator must have the skills and maturity to handle this, and the parties concerned must have confidence in the mediator. Maybe there is someone – a friend, a colleague, an elder in the church – who would mediate for you.

Three members of a team were feeling very frustrated. Their grievances had been aired at an annual review and the team leader had met with each of them. However, they felt nothing had been resolved. We were booked to do some teambuilding with them, but realised that the conflict needed resolution before any constructive teambuilding could begin.

We talked with each of the three members individually, listening to what they felt about the situation. We then met with the leader. Finally, with everyone together, we tried to draw out each person's feelings and frustrations in a constructive way, ensuring that all the others heard what he or she was saying. Agreement was reached and procedures set up to ensure better communication and conflict resolution.

## Practical ways of resolving conflict

1 Admit the problem, don't brush it under the carpet.
2 Set a good time to discuss the problem; not when one or the other is tired or under pressure from other sources.
3 Define the problem clearly. Keep to the one issue – don't drag up all your other grievances.
4 Tackle the problem, not the person. Avoid 'you' statements and accusations, and 'always' and 'never'.
5 Try to see the other person's viewpoint. Perhaps someone else, who is not so emotionally involved in the outcome, could explain her position to you more clearly.
6 Accept responsibility for your actions. Making excuses for your behaviour and blaming others for theirs doesn't solve disputes. Own up to your part in the problem. 'I should have said something to you as soon as I heard . . .'
7 Solve the problem jointly; look at different possible solutions together. The agreed solution should have the benefit of both perspectives. Aim for one that you can both accept.
8 Commit yourself to making the agreed solution work, not – 'This was agreed but I was never really happy with it.' Forget your original position. The new agreement is paramount. Make it work.

Here is a diagrammatic representation handling conflict.

Conflict > >    Confront problem > >    Forgive > >
                face the truth           no revenge
                acknowledge reality      good attitudes

> > Resolve or win    > > Growth in self/relationship
                yield
                compromise
                withdraw . . . if resolution
                                impracticable/impossible

We have now examined the interpersonal elements of being a team: Expectations and assumptions, Commitment, Communication, Conflict.

# INDIVIDUAL ACTIVITIES

**1** Try to identify your own conflict style preference from the descriptions. Do you use this inappropriately? Can you develop the use of other styles?

**2** Have you an unresolved conflict in your life? Have you faced up to it and sought resolution or have you tried to win, yield, compromise or withdraw inappropriately? Consider how you can reach a greater degree of resolution.

# TEAM ACTIVITIES

**1** Discuss all the team members' preferred conflict styles and how they impinge on each other.

**2** Discuss how you as a team can handle conflict better. Is there opportunity for members to bring differences of opinion forward for discussion?

**3** Your team meetings take place once a month. Some of you feel these meetings are not very inspiring and you attend only as a chore. Some would like them to be more businesslike with a prepared agenda and more effective use of the time. Others would like more opportunity to pray for each other and share problems. What is the way forward? How can the team meetings be altered to meet these different aspirations and thus increase the effectiveness of the team?

Role play the above:

a) play it badly (each using preferred style exclusively!)

b) play it using the 8 practical ways of resolving conflict.

**4** Do you have a mediation procedure? Discuss the possibility of using a mediator to help resolve conflicts.

This brings us to the end of Section 2.

# SECTION 3: INDIVIDUAL ASPECTS OF TEAMWORK

## Personality type *Chapter 8*

Understanding people
... personality types
   ... Myers Briggs Type Indicator
     ... we need each other
       ... problem solving as a team
         ... different ways of communicating
           ... different working environments
             ... different lifestyles.

## Gifts and abilities *Chapter 9*

We all have gifts
... finding our gifts
   ... using our gifts in the team
     ... complementing not competing
       ... link between energy and gifts
         ... God's rules for using our gifts
           ... recognising others' gifts.

## Team roles *Chapter 10*

Teamwork research
... identifying roles
   ... team leader role
     ... successful teams
       ... roles in the early church.

# 8

# Personality type

## Perspectives

A colleague of ours was stationary in a line of traffic in Mexico City. The car in front very slowly rolled back and nudged his front bumper. At this the driver got out and began to berate our colleague for running into his back bumper! Obviously they saw things from different perspectives. Our different views of life can easily lead to misunderstanding, since we all see things from our own perspective.

In the New Testament very different personalities were sometimes called to work together. Consider Paul and Timothy. Paul was an outspoken, strong-minded firebrand. Timothy must have been a much less confident person as his timidity is referred to more than once. Paul had obviously learnt to understand Timothy quite well. He tells the Corinthians, 'If Timothy comes, see to it that he has nothing to fear while he is with you' (1 Corinthians 16:10). Paul seems to have been sensitive to Timothy's personality, and wanted the Corinthians to be sensitive too.

## Understanding people

Understanding how another person 'ticks' goes a long way towards helping you get on together. Also, the better you understand yourself, the better you may be able to understand, and even appreciate, how you differ from the other person, or in what ways you are like him.

We sometimes say two people are incompatible or have a personality clash. By this we mean that they are so different that they simply cannot get on. It is true that it takes us longer to understand and relate to people very different from ourselves. This can set sparks flying if we are in a team with them. However, if we work at it, it's probable that we will learn to appreciate them, perhaps *because* they are different. In teamwork we need different perspectives, different styles and different approaches.

In theory, we all agree that these differences give interest and variety, that they add spice to life. In practice, we often find the spice overpowering! Other people can be so different that we find it hard to accept them, to discover anything we can agree about. Understanding personality types, our own and other people's, helps us accept that there is no right or wrong; that each different personality is as valid as any other.

## Personality type

Attempts to measure and analyse personality go back at least as far as Hippocrates with the Hippocratic medical view of personality linked to the body fluids: Sanguine, Choleric, Phlegmatic, and Melancholic. Since then, there have been many other attempts to describe and explain differences in human behaviour by classifying personality types.

A popular personality measure is the Myers Briggs Type Indicator (MBTI). This is increasingly being used in both secular and Christian circles for management purposes – to help develop teamwork and other interpersonal skills.

It is important to realise that the MBTI measures *preferences*. We each have a preferred style and will not *always* behave or react in certain ways. Some people worry that the theory of type puts people in boxes and somehow limits them. This is not so when it is used correctly; indeed the opposite can be true. By discovering our preferred style and strengths, we can also recognise our weaknesses and try to work on them, so that we become stronger in those areas.

# Myers Briggs Type Indicator

The full indicator, published by Consulting Psychologists Press, needs professional scoring. Kiersey and Bates have a shorter measure[1] which you can score yourself. Details of some publications on personality type and the MBTI can be found in the Resources section on page 156.

We will look briefly at the four main parameters on which the Myers Briggs work is based, which explain the differences in human behaviour.

(E) Extraversion _____ Introversion (I)

Which is your preferred world of activity? Is it the inner world of ideas and concepts (Introversion) or the outer world of people and things (Extraversion)? The introvert is territorial and likes a reasonable degree of privacy. The extravert is much more sociable and is happy with a far greater degree of social interaction. An extravert may want to go to a party to relax whereas the introvert may need to escape from the party in order to relax. The extravert likes activity and uses 'trial and error' methods. The introvert likes to think more deeply before taking action.

(S) Sensing _____ Intuition (N)

Which is your preferred way of taking in information and data? Do you use only your senses (eyes, ears, nose and so on) or do you also use your intuition? Sensing people usually notice details, the colour of people's eyes, what they wear and the like. They are down-to-earth, sensible, practical, in touch with reality and live very much for today. Those who have an intuitive preference easily forget names and details, but see whole truths and concepts. Intuitives are speculative, inspirational and imaginative and often live in the future. The absent-minded professor is an extreme case of an intuitive. If the sensing people see the trees, the intuitives see the wood.

(T) Thinking _____ Feeling (F)

How we make decisions is the third continuum. Our preference can be to do this on the basis of impersonal logic, analysis and objectivity (Thinking) or on the basis of values, personal feelings and allowing for circumstances (Feeling). Those who prefer feeling judgments prize harmony and are often seen as warm and trusting individuals. Those who prefer thinking judgments are often seen as logical and firm and are more prone to scepticism.

(J) Judging ———————————————— Perceiving (P)

This fourth continuum has to do with our preferred style of living. Those with a judging preference like closure, that is, things settled and decided; those with a perceiving preference like to keep matters open and undecided until all data for a decision is available. Those with a perceiving preference have a more flexible, spontaneous lifestyle and may be described as fun-loving. Those with a judging preference have a more planned, regulated lifestyle and are work oriented.

The first and last parameters are called attitudes (I/E P/J). The second and third parameters are called functions (S/N T/F). (Intuition is designated by the letter N to avoid confusion with introversion). The MBTI shows our preference on each of the above four parameters, and at the end of this chapter there is a brief description of the sixteen possible personality types yielded by this result.

## WHAT DOES THIS TEACH US ABOUT TEAMWORK?

Understanding personality types can help your interpersonal skills. Other people will not necessarily think and behave as you do, and you should not expect them to. You can learn to understand and accept their differences – their ways of thinking and behaving, the things they feel are important, their unique function as part of the body of Christ.

We need each other. The Lord has not given any one of us a fully balanced personality. For example, intuitives can help sensing types to see new possibilities and prepare for the future, whereas sensing types can help intuitives to take notice of the details they might otherwise miss, and to be aware of what needs doing here and now. The feeling types on your team can help the thinkers to be aware of how other people will feel about and react to the decisions they take. The thinkers can help the feelers to be consistent in their decision making.

You need people in the team who are not the same as you. If you find yourself in a team with someone who is opposite to you on all four preferences, you may have special problems in understanding each other. Nonetheless, it can be done, and the Lord will help.

## Everyone uses all four attitudes (Introversion/Extraversion and Judging/Perception)

We can be introvert and extravert, and use both attitudes, depending on the situation. If you prefer the planned, judging lifestyle, you can be flexible when necessary. If you prefer the spontaneous lifestyle, you still find it possible to organise yourself. You simply prefer one way over the other.

## Everyone uses all four functions (Sensing/Intuition and Thinking/Feeling)

We all gather information by using our senses and our intuition, but we have a preference for one way and will, therefore, have developed its use better. We all make decisions using both the thinking and the feeling functions. We simply have a preference for one and tend to use it more often.

## Type development

Type theory[2] says that, while we use all four functions, we have a dominant, an auxiliary, a tertiary and an inferior function. The dominant function is our true and trusted friend that we develop in childhood (6–12 years). We then develop our auxiliary function in our teens (12–20 years) and our tertiary function in our twenties to mid thirties (20–35 years). We develop our least preferred function, the inferior function, from our mid-thirties to fifty or so (35–50 years). The inferior function is the one we are least adept at using. Developing its use is one possible explanation for the midlife struggles many people experience.

The order of development of function preference for each of the sixteen types is listed along with the type descriptions at the end of this chapter.

## A model for problem solving

Type development can be used in problem solving both individually and as a team. All the four functions are needed and usually in the following order:

1 SENSING (S) – to determine the facts and examine the details.
2 INTUITION (N) – to look at the possibilities and options.
3 THINKING (T) – to examine the logical effects of these options.
4 FEELING (F) – to see how feelings and values will be affected.

1 Those whose dominant function is sensing can help the team to marshal the facts: What really is the problem? What has been done so far?, etc.
2 The dominant intuitives can then propose the possibilities: In what other ways could this problem be looked at? What similar problems have we dealt with before?, etc.
3 The dominant thinking types can then ask: What are the pros and cons of the possibilities suggested? What would be the cost of each solution?, etc.
4 Finally, dominant feeling types can contribute the likely reactions of the people concerned and the values involved.

## Different types prefer different ways of communicating

Communication within the team is vitally important – so important that we've devoted a whole chapter to it. If you can understand the MBTI preferences of the other members of the team, especially as contrasted with your own, it should help you to communicate with them in ways that they will understand. It should also help you to understand what they wish to communicate to you. Our type affects our preferred communication style.

Extravert members of the team probably like to talk, to talk fast, with energy and enthusiasm. They like communicating in groups, and communicating face-to-face. Their introverted team mates probably like to think before speaking, and prefer to communicate one-to-one rather than in a group. They may even like to communicate in writing rather than through speech. Extraverts may need to beware of dominating discussion, introverts may need to learn to be assertive with their opinions.

The sensing members of your team will choose to use specific examples, the intuitives are likely to refer to general concepts. Sensing types will like straightforward suggestions which are obviously possible, while the intuitives will prefer unusual and imaginative suggestions.

Thinkers and feelers also differ in their communication styles. Thinkers prefer to be precise and to the point, while feelers are more concerned to be chatty and friendly. If you need to convince the thinking members of your team, use reasoned logic. You will more easily convince the feeling members by enthusiasm and by stressing the personal aspects of your argument.

When presenting your own views or putting forward your arguments, those of you who prefer judging will tend to state your case clearly and decisively. However, those of you with a perceptive preference may put forward your views much more tentatively.

## Different types prefer different working environments

Another difference highlighted by temperament type is that of our preferred working environment. Obviously this may have quite a bearing on how you divide up the team's tasks.

Extravert members often actually like interruptions such as phone calls, especially if they are working on a long and monotonous job! They prefer to have other people around them as they work and they like lots of variety and activity in their work. They tend to work well in groups and their ideas spring from discussion. Introverted members of the team, however, will not take kindly to interruptions, including phone calls, when they are trying to concentrate on a job in hand. They will happily work away at one job even if it takes a long time and they are working on it alone. They need quiet, solitary periods of time to think things through.

Those who have a sensing preference will not be excited by learning new skills. They tend to prefer to work at activities where they already feel competent. They can be relied on to have their facts correct and are careful with the details of their work. They are often most at home doing practical tasks. If they have an imaginative or inspirational idea they may ignore it. Intuitives, on the other hand, tend to love learning new skills, but may lose interest once they have mastered something. They are always looking for innovations. They are inclined to make errors of fact, and are more interested in the overall concept than the details. They are the ones with most of the inspirational ideas and they trust in these ideas and act on them.

Those whose decision-making preference is thinking tend to be firm-minded in work. They may be so single-minded that they are able to work within a less than harmonious environment. They may unwittingly hurt colleagues' feelings, as they tend to stick to the principles involved and do not always consider other people's views. Feelers, on the other hand, find it hard to concentrate on work unless there is harmony around them. They have difficulty in confronting others or telling them things they may not want to hear. They tend not to be logically decisive and their judgments may be swayed by their own and/or others' feelings.

Team members who prefer the judging lifestyle need to be able to plan their work and function best when they have a definite schedule to keep to. They finish projects they undertake. They tend to make decisions quickly, sometimes without considering all the options, but they are reliable and follow tasks through. Those who prefer the perceptive lifestyle are not so keen on planning their work. They like to be flexible. They may put off unpleasant jobs and postpone decisions, but they adapt well to change and are open to new ideas.

It does take some time to master and understand particular personality models such as Myers Briggs, and you may find it helpful to do a training course on MBTI or read some of the books on the subject, listed in the Resources section on pages 156–159. You may be familiar with a model other than MBTI and want to use that one instead. What is important is that you take account of personality difference in your teambuilding. We have found understanding personality type to be a very helpful teambuilding tool.

## INDIVIDUAL ACTIVITIES

1 Write down the six characteristics that describe your personality best. If the Myers Briggs model has proved valuable, use that to help you.
2 What reactions, both positive and negative, could other people have to these characteristics? For example, *thoroughness* – useful when care and precision are required (keeping the records straight), could be seen as nitpicking and perfectionism by the more creative types.
3 Try to describe your preferred communication style and your preferred work environment.
4 What particular strengths do you bring when solving problems? What are your weaknesses?

## TEAM ACTIVITIES

1 Each of you tell the others what you see as your own personality characteristics (from 1 above) and the positive and negative impact you think they have on the team (from 2 above). Does the team agree with your assessment?
2 Explain your preferred ways of communicating, eg:
'I like to discuss things together in the group. It helps me to articulate my thoughts and come to a decision' or 'I prefer to talk with each one of you individually and find out your feelings on an issue, and have time to reflect on these before I come to a conclusion.'

3 Discuss your preferred working environments and how you can best accommodate these in your teamwork.

4 Play the Zin obelisk game (Exercise 2 page 163) and see if you can observe how the different personalities in the team work together to solve the problem.

5 Role play the following: your team is the home committee of an organisation sending people to distribute food and clothing to refugee families. The leader of a team in Africa is asking for a decision about whether to abort the work and return home because of the fighting. The team out there is very divided about this and some members will be disappointed if they have to come home at this stage.

As the home committee responsible, consider the facts, possible options, the effect of these options on team members, on other agencies, governments, etc. What feelings and values (of supporters, home team members, African team members) are likely to be affected by different possible decisions? Try to come to an agreed course of action.

# ADDENDUM TO CHAPTER EIGHT

## The sixteen temperament types

By indicating our preference on each of these four parameters using the initial letters, we produce a four letter code for each of the sixteen temperament types.

Extravert (E) _____ Introvert (I)
Sensing (S) _____ Intuitive (N)
Thinking (T) _____ Feeling (F)
Judging (J) _____ Perceiving (P)

**INTJ** – self-confident, decisive, pragmatic, brainstormers, analytical, independent, single-minded, theoretical ... love challenges that require creative thinking, often rise to positions of responsibility, take organisational goals seriously ... often found in scientific research, engineering...

**INTP** – precise, logical, intellectual, diligent, reserved and impersonal ... difficult to get to know, precise in thought and language, concentrate well, seek to understand the universe, often work alone ... often specialise in philosophy, architecture, mathematics, university lecturing...

**INFJ** – complicated and complex, perfectionist, imaginative, vulnerable, warm, original ... strong drive to help others, enjoy studying, high integrity, good interpersonal relations yet hard to get to know really well ... often become psychiatrists, doctors, writers...

**INFP** – loyal, idealistic, reticent, adaptable, honourable ... facility with languages, welcome new ideas, avoid conflict, keep their word, not good decision makers, profound sense of honour, like autonomy ... often found in Christian ministry or missionary work, psychology...

**ENTJ** – empirical, objective, dynamic, organised, hard working ... can take hard decisions, intolerant of inefficiency, natural leaders, strongly driven to succeed, harness people to goals, expect a great deal from their spouses ... often found in managerial positions, organisational leadership...

**ENTP** – ingenious, inspirational, resourceful, innovative, entrepreneurial ... natural people managers, like taking risks, respond well in crises, like to beat the system, rely on improvisation, natural conversationalists, like variety ... make good management consultants, inventors...

**ENFJ** – cooperative, influential, people-orientated, socially adept, even tempered and tolerant, caring, trusting ... can handle complex data, natural group leaders, know others' needs, may overextend themselves, can be idealistic in relationships, devoted spouses, long for the ideal ... make good actors/actresses, high level salespeople, executives...

**ENFP** – imaginative, ingenious, warmly enthusiastic, credible, optimistic, charming, emotional, creative ... sense significance of events, very observant, easily bored, personalise work, good communicators, like freedom of action, poor on detail and follow-through ... make good journalists, salespeople, play/screen writers...

**ISTJ** – serious, orderly, dependable, persevering, thorough, stable, faithful, unpretentious ... support the status quo, keep the rules, their word is their bond, conserve resources, like consistent behaviour in self and others ... often found in banking, clerical, legal professions. . .

**ISTP** – impulsive, fearless, egalitarian, flamboyant, cheerful, active . . . dislike obligations, thrive on excitement, easily bored, not good scholars, may ignore rules, keen on tools, poor verbal skills . . . make good artisans, drivers, laboratory technicians. . .

**ISFJ** – responsible, dependable, hardworking, loyal . . . primary desire is to serve others, work is good and play must be earned, good homemakers, dislike supervising others, value traditions, relate best to those who need them, may take on too much . . . make good nurses, teachers, secretaries, middle managers. . .

**ISFP** – independent, sensitive, retiring, kind, sympathetic, optimistic, cheerful, modest . . . dislike arguments, live in the here and now, do not prepare and plan, value their hunches, keenly tuned senses, inclined to fine arts, love animals . . . found in a wide variety of occupations but especially gifted as dancers, painters, composers. . .

**ESTJ** – punctual, responsible, matter of fact, consistent, dependable, neat, orderly . . . pillars of the community, outstanding organisers, enjoy traditions and rituals, may not be responsive to feelings and views of others, keep rules and expect others to do so . . . found in positions of responsibility in many fields as administrators. . .

**ESTP** – resourceful, sophisticated, active, witty, adventurous, charming, unpredictable, popular . . . good party people, seek excitement, make things happen, like the good life, live in the here and now, lots of friends . . . make outstanding negotiators, troubleshooters, administrative fire fighters, entrepreneurs. . .

**ESFJ** – warm-hearted, talkative, orderly, conscientious, softhearted . . . most sociable of all types, harmony is treasured and worked for, supporters of home/school/church, excellent hosts, attend to the needs of others, need to be appreciated, expect others to follow the system, may be fearful . . . often in people to people jobs such as selling, preaching, teaching. . .

**ESFP** – optimistic, easy-going, generous, happy, adaptable, hedonistic . . . may be self-indulgent, attractive to others, low tolerance for anxiety, rely on personal experience, enjoy dramatic situations . . . often found in public relations, selling, entertainment industry. . .

## The order of development of function preference for each type

| | |
|---|---|
| Extravert (E) | Introvert (I) |
| Sensing (S) | Intuitive (N) |
| Thinking (T) | Feeling (F) |
| Judging (J) | Perceiving (P) |

Below is the function development order for each type. An INTJ, for example, has intuition as the dominant function, thinking as the auxiliary, feeling as the tertiary and sensing as the inferior function.

| | | | |
|---|---|---|---|
| INTJ...N>T>F>S | ENTJ...T>N>S>F | ISTJ...S>T>F>N | ESTJ...T>S>N>F |
| INTP...T>N>S>F | ENTP...N>T>F>S | ISTP...T>S>N>F | ESTP...S>T>F>N |
| INFJ...N>F>T>S | ENFJ...F>N>S>T | ISFJ...S>F>T>N | ESFJ...F>S>N>T |
| INFP...F>N>S>T | ENFP...N>S>T>S | ISFP...F>S>N>T | ESFP...S>F>T>N |

Note: part of this chapter has been adapted from Chapter six of *Naturally Gifted*.

# *9*

# Gifts and abilities

## We all have gifts

You are gifted. Discovering the gifts God has given you individually, and the way these fit in with the gifts of the rest of the team, should help you all work together effectively. The gifts and abilities of the team members are the component parts of the team. A balanced team, where there is a broad spectrum of gifts and abilities, is one of the signs of a good team, as we mentioned in Chapter 3.

In God's eyes everyone is of inestimable worth. He considered us worth dying for. He really values us and therefore we should value ourselves, and one another. Each of us is a very important person.

## Purposeful living

God has created us for a purpose. This is the logical outcome of believing there is a creator and that we are not the product of some random coming together of atoms and molecules. Discovering your particular gifts and linking them to God's purpose for you is exciting and rewarding. It is also rewarding to discover your place in the body, in the team, as you discern how your gifts fit in with the gifts God has given to the other team members.

Faith Forster[1] says ' "All that I am" . . . there is a fulness in that phrase which suggests every part of my personality and being, my abilities, interests, values, giftings . . . a very important person! ... Not as egocentric as it sounds. To discover who I am and what gifting God has given me is to honour my creator and to acknowledge and to cooperate with his handiwork in me. Even if he then calls me to give myself up to martyrdom or (which is possibly harder!) to lay down my life in undramatic daily acts of service to others, I will know the value of what I am laying down.'

If God values us so greatly that he took the trouble to create us as uniquely gifted individuals, we should take notice of this. Let's find out what our gifts are and how they can best be used in the team.

## Finding your natural gifts

There are many ways to help you determine your gifts. The work of the psychologist John Holland has formed the basis of some of the world's most popular occupational interest tests. These make the assumption that we are interested in things in which we are gifted, and that we find job satisfaction in using these gifts.

The Interest test in *Naturally Gifted*[2] will identify your interest themes for you. However, many of you can probably identify the areas in which you are gifted simply by reading the interest theme descriptions in Exercise 8 (page 181).

## USING THE TEAM'S DIFFERENT GIFTS IS EFFECTIVE

We have proved this for ourselves. We work very closely together. Neither of us would be willing to do the travelling we do and take on the tasks we do on our own. Between us we have a much broader range of gifts and abilities to meet the challenges we face. Our team of two has grown stronger over the years. We are now able to achieve things together which neither of us could achieve alone. Writing books is one of them!

We have seen many instances of different gifts being used in a team. The members of one Bible translation team we visited were coping well with living in rural Africa, and were building excellent relationships with the local people. However, they were struggling with all the 'deskwork' involved in the technical side of the translation task. A young analytical linguist joined the team temporarily and with her help they were able to make excellent progress in this area.

Another translation team was strong on the technical deskwork but was struggling with the amount of liaison needed with local church leaders and officials. The members also found the practicalities of third world rural life very draining and time consuming. For example, the water supply would fail, the Land Rover would need mending and a host of other irritants would come along. When the team was enlarged to include some people who were able to handle the practical jobs and enjoy the people-related tasks, the academically-minded couple were freed to concentrate on the linguistic and translation work.

## Competition and jealousy

It is easy to write about complementing each other's gifts and appreciating our differences. It makes sense to us. In practice, we know how amazingly easy it is for people to be jealous of each other's gifts and to try to compete.

When working with a team where each member so obviously needs the other, we often hear someone say, 'He/she is so much more able than I am.' Then when we talk to the other person he or she often says the same thing! Each feels threatened by his or her colleague's competences. How much better to try to appreciate one another. It is God who gives us someone on the team who has more gifts than we do in a particular area. A person often marries his opposite because he instinctively knows that this person complements him. Even so, spouses often compete with each other.

Some of the successful teams we know are composed of opposites. They laugh about how different they are and about some of the misunderstandings that occurred when they began working together. Now that they have learnt to be a team they really appreciate each other. They can happily comment about how good their team mate is at some task they cannot do.

## Energy and gifts

Work activities we engage in use differing amounts of energy, linked to our skill areas as follows.

i Natural skills – these are easy and relaxing, even energising to use.

ii Learned skills – we have been trained to use these adequately, but they use more energy than natural skills.

iii Non-skills – we struggle with these because they do not come naturally to us, and we are not trained to use them. They drain our energy.

The majority of our work should use our natural skills. If our work demands that we use non-skills more than sixty per cent of the time then we use too much energy. This is confirmed by the scriptural injunction on how to use our gifts: 'If a man's gift is serving, let him serve, if it is teaching, let him teach' (Romans 12:7). We work best when we use our God-given gifts, rather than struggle to achieve in our non-skill areas.

## God's rules for using our gifts

God has laid down certain rules for using the gifts he has given us, and these have important implications for teamwork. Our focus should be on the giver, not the gifts. This does not mean that you should despise your gifts. On the contrary, you should value them as something precious given to you by God.

In the New Testament, spiritual and natural gifts are not clearly distinguished from one another. Prophesying, serving, teaching, encouraging, contributing to others, giving, leadership, and showing mercy are all found together. There appears to be no clear distinction between the natural gifts, which may be found in any person, and the spiritual gifts which you would expect to find only in a Christian. Spiritual gifts are the manifestation of the Holy Spirit (1 Corinthians 12:7).

Our own experience is that when we submit ourselves to God, he takes our natural gifts and makes them spiritual. It is interesting that the chapter in Romans on gifts begins with the exhortation, 'Offer your bodies as living sacrifices' (Romans 12:1), and tells us this is our spiritual service.

Using our gifts effectively requires faith. We need to have our eyes on God, not on ourselves. In Romans 12:3, speaking of gifts, Paul says, 'Do not think of yourself more highly than you ought, but rather think of yourself with sober judgment, in accordance with the measure of faith God has given you.' We each need to have a realistic estimate of ourself. It is even more important to remember that it is God's giving, his grace, that is at the root of all our gifting. This perspective should help us to exercise the faith we need to use our gifts.

That said, there are two major pitfalls we should beware of. The first is to think we have no gifts, the second is to think we have the best gifts. Neither is true. None of us is without gifts, and the gifts we have are the gifts that God has given us, that we may serve him as he determines.

## What motivates you?

Your motivation for using your gifts is important. Some people use their gifts purely to satisfy themselves and to make themselves feel fulfilled. Using your gifts will help you to find fulfilment, but your primary motivation should be to bring glory to God through serving others. 'Each one should use whatever gift he has received to serve others' (1 Peter 4:10). When people tell us that they feel their gifts are not being used, we sometimes say, 'Try giving them away. That's why they're there.' Are you frustrated? Do you feel your gifts are overlooked? Start using them to serve others. Each member of the body of Christ belongs to the other members (Romans 12:5). This is strong language – we are inextricably linked together. If you are not using your gifts to serve others then you are denying them something God has provided for them through you.

## Recognising and valuing others' gifts

Not only does the Bible teach us that we should use our gifts to serve our fellow Christians, it also teaches us to appreciate their gifts. If they need your gifts, you need theirs too.

> Now the body is not made up of one part but of many. If the foot should say, 'Because I am not a hand, I do not belong to the body,' it would not for that reason cease to be part of the body. And if the ear should say, 'Because I am not an eye, I do not belong to the body,' it would not for that reason cease to be part of the body. If the whole body were an eye, where would the sense of hearing be? If the whole body were an ear, where would the sense of smell be?
>
> *1 Corinthians 12:14–17*

Yet how easily most of us slip into honouring or elevating one gift above another. Within a congregation, we can be tempted to honour those exercising the more upfront, 'spiritual' gifts of teaching, preaching or prophesying, and fail to notice those with gifts of encouraging, serving, or showing mercy. In our local church magazine one month, there was a note thanking by name those who clean the church toilets. How seldom we remember to thank *all* those who serve us – in making the coffee, arranging the flowers, hoovering the room, putting out the songbooks, etc. It is too easy to give all the affirmation to the pastor, or the visiting preacher, and miss out those who minister to us in other ways.

To accord equal honour is not the way of the secular world, but it is an integral part of God's upside-down kingdom. We must try to discern, use and honour one another's gifts in the team.

## INDIVIDUAL ACTIVITIES

1 See if you can identify your natural gifts by using the interest theme descriptions in Exercise 8, page 181.

**2** Write down the areas in which you are weak (not gifted) and could benefit from other team members' help, eg computing, practical (cars/machines).

**3** List your strengths. How can you help other team members by using your gifts? Eg designing publicity material (artistic).

## TEAM ACTIVITIES

**1** Make a chart on which each team member marks their interest codes (see Exercise 8). You will find it helpful to use different coloured pencils (see diagram on page 98).

   i Do you complement each other?

  ii How do the codes match the team tasks? Are there particular aspects of the team goals being unmet for which one of you has natural gifts?

 iii Is the team well balanced, or are some interests that the team needs missing?

**2** Discuss how you can complement each other by using each one's gifts to the full. Bear in mind particularly the team's goals. For instance, a team formed to produce a magazine might be:

> Fred – computing (general, some programming, etc)
> Anne – administration, including typing and general organising
> David – proofreading (he is meticulous)
> Bill – artistic flair, magazine editing

**3** Does each of you feel that your gifts are valued and used in the team?

**For example:**

| Fred | CRS | ———————— |
| Anne | ESC | ———— |
| David | CRE | – – – – – |
| Gill | ASC | –·–·–·–·– |

Realistic
Investigative
Artistic
Social
Enterprising
Conventional

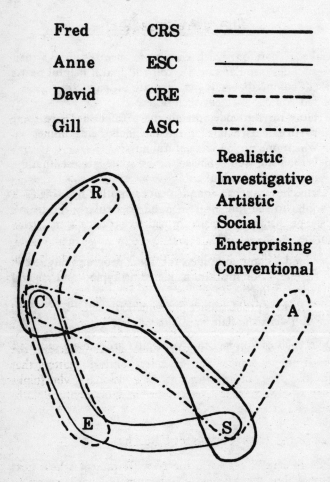

# 10

# Team roles

The centre-forward may have another role besides his playing position in the football team. He may be the captain, responsible for providing leadership. The goalkeeper may, off the field, be the 'life and soul of the party', someone who helps the team relax and socialise. Such additional roles, distinct from the functional ones of centre-forward and goalkeeper, may be just as important for the success of the team.

You are probably on a team by virtue of your skills or your job. Perhaps you are an expert in a particular field, or have a particular area of responsibility. For example, you may be the treasurer, the personnel supervisor, or the secretary. This is your functional role on the team.

However, you are also fulfilling other roles in the team whether or not you are aware of it – team roles which are more linked to your personality type than to your job or your skills. You may be a natural diplomat and therefore the obvious one to handle any delicate 'political' matters that arise. Another team member may be a visionary who thinks up new approaches, and yet another may be a natural gatherer of resources.

## Roles in the New Testament Church

There are several places in the New Testament where gifts are listed, but the passage in Ephesians (4:11–12) seems to be somewhat different in kind. In fact, some commentators say that the delineation of apostles, prophets, evangelists, pastors and teachers refers to office, not gifting. Perhaps the list refers to roles – for example the role of the apostle being to go out and break new ground, or the role of the pastor being to care for and nurture the flock. Barnabas acted as an apostle when he went on missionary journeys with Paul. He also had the roles of pastor and teacher. Earlier, he fulfilled all three roles when he went to Paul after his conversion, showed him acceptance and understanding, and taught him about the Christian faith.

## Research into teamwork

Dr Meredith Belbin, of the Industrial Training Research Unit at Cambridge, undertook some research to try to answer two questions, why are some management teams more successful than others, and what makes up a successful team? For the research, the Administrative Staff College at Henley was used as a laboratory over a seven year period. The results, published in 1981, have been the most important single contribution of the past decade to our understanding of how teams work, and how to make them work better. Conclusions have emerged that have much wider application than simply to management teams.

## Research findings

Teams were observed as they tackled various tasks that were set for them, and their success or otherwise was closely monitored. The implications of the research results were then tried out in actual companies and in a variety of team situations, and were shown to work. Since then, the research has been translated into a number of languages and its conclusions widely applied.

The research findings identified why some teams were more successful than others. Eventually it also became possible to predict which teams would be successful by using personality tests to examine the mix of personalities in the team.

Good management teams are formed when the correct mix of personalities is brought together. Sometimes a manager who has been very successful in one team, proves less so when transferred to another team – perhaps because the necessary 'chemistry' between the team members is lacking. The Henley research also showed that there are identifiable team roles that may be adopted, and that the right combination is needed for the team to function well. Too many of one role and not enough of another leads to an ineffective team.

## Identifying roles

In successful teams, members contribute in two dimensions: in their functional role (their job) and in their team role (style of interacting). Both are important. Most members can, and often do, fit more than one team role, and it is possible for a person to develop into some roles that are not his first choice, so long as they are compatible with his personality. Success in a team depends not only on having the right people in each functional role but also on correctly identifying their team roles – and applying this knowledge.

Teams work best when they recognise the need for specific roles and try to ensure that these roles are played within the team. An individual's effectiveness as a team member depends on recognising and adapting to the roles needed. Each individual is suited to certain team roles and unsuited to others by virtue of his personal characteristics. If there is no natural visionary in the team, merely appointing other members to a think-tank will not fill the gap, unless at least one of them has the necessary attributes.

At this point, before you read the following descriptions, you may like to turn to the Self perception inventory in Exercise 9 (page 184) to see what your team role/s is likely to be.

## THE TEAM LEADER ROLES

Of the eight team roles identified in the Henley research, two were found to be appropriate to team leadership. It is particularly important to have someone with the right cluster of personality characteristics as overall team leader.

## Coordinator

The first team leader role is that of Coordinator. Having interpersonal skills is probably the most important characteristic of Coordinator team leaders. They need to be able to work with all kinds of people and have an aptitude for organising them. They use their interpersonal skills to achieve agreement in the team. Coordinators are not necessarily unusually academically gifted – it was found best if they were about equal to their team mates, but not far ahead of them – nor do they need to be exceptionally creative.

Coordinators can see both sides in a disagreement and enjoy reconciling different points of view. They are likely to be fairly assertive but also capable of responding to others' needs, and able to make decisions acceptable to all the team members. Coordinators control the team members effectively, and, at the same time, skilfully use the resources of the group.

The Coordinator type of leader suits a balanced team; that is, one that contains team members functioning in all eight roles. However, Coordinators' weaknesses are a tendency to be lazy if they can find someone else to do the work, and taking the praise for what was actually a team effort. (Originally this role was termed Chairman but later changed to Coordinator, which we prefer.)

## Shaper

While the Henley research showed the Coordinator to be the classic team leader, in the real world many successful team leaders have a very different personality profile. This other type of leader has been termed a Shaper.

In many ways Shapers are the opposite of what we would think of as team people, in that they may be argumentative, and are often aggressive and impatient. They seem to enjoy conflict. Their motivation is to win at any cost. Shapers like to have a strong influence on group decisions, and may be willing to be unpopular in order to get their views across. They are happy to take the lead when action is required, and their major role is to shape the way the team effort is applied. Shapers are resilient and fearless but may overreact to disappointments. Their personality is inclined to drive them and the group they lead into action, as they direct attention to the setting of objectives and priorities.

The Shaper leader tends to lead in a directive way and does best with a group that is prone to complacency or inaction. However, a Shaper leader can disrupt a well-balanced team, if he is inclined to irritability and/or easily frustrated. Shapers are slow to apologise when they are wrong. Where a Shaper is a member of the team rather than the leader, he needs the sort of guidance that a spirited thoroughbred requires.

## OTHER TEAM ROLES

Other team roles were termed the Plant, the Resource Investigator, the Implementer, the Monitor Evaluator, the Team Worker and the Completer. The characteristics of these team roles are as follows.

### Plant

Plants are usually intelligent and creative people. Their major role in the team is to come up with new ideas and strategies. They produce original suggestions but are also capable of thinking of possible new solutions to long-standing problems.

Plants take an independent and innovative look at most situations, and see patterns where others see only unconnected items. This gives them the ability to rearrange ideas and techniques in order to achieve desired outcomes. Within the team, Plants will either 'flower' or they won't. This depends on whether their team role is recognised and harnessed by the leader. Conflict can arise if there is more than one Plant in a team, because then there may be too many ideas and uncertainty as to whose ideas it would be best to follow.

Plants' weaknesses are that they neglect practical matters: they are preoccupied with ideas, and find it hard to cooperate because they prefer to keep their ideas to themselves.

## Resource Investigator

Resource Investigators can appear similar to Plants in that they are also ideas people. However, their ideas come from outside themselves and often from outside the group (hence their title). Both Plants and Resource Investigators are innovators, and occasionally the same person can occupy both roles, but usually the roles are complementary. Both roles are needed in the team.

Resource Investigators are able to relate to people; but more than that, they are able to see the possibilities in situations and relationships and follow them up. They tend to have a broad range of personal contacts, and, therefore, access to people with specialist knowledge when this is required. Not only do they explore ideas and possibilities, they can usually also sell these ideas to the rest of the team, and conduct any subsequent negotiations. However, Resource Investigators can be vulnerable to losing their initial enthusiasm and failing to follow through.

A team needs both types of creativity – that which the Plant supplies, and that which the Resourve Investigator supplies. It is important that the team makes use of the best ideas generated. To a large extent this probably depends on the leadership of the team. Correct balance of the rest of the roles is also important.

## Implementer

Implementers work for the good of the organisation. A team with a high proportion of Implementers tends to do well. Implementers are dependable and stable, even when under pressure, and can be relied on to see a job through. They are disciplined and have an orderly approach to work, striving to do the job properly and to meet targets.

Implementers are good organisers, seeing, of course, how to implement ideas and concepts into practical working procedures. They may, in fact, be more interested in practicalities than in new ideas, but they have a talent for sorting out the concrete steps that must be taken in order to use good ideas.

Implementers are strong characters, able to take action that is unpopular, since they put the good of the organisation before their personal desires. Despite their own self-discipline they are tolerant of others, but being respecters of the established way of looking at things, do not tend to generate creativity. Their weakness springs from this tendency to obstruct change. (This role was originally termed the Company Worker.)

## Monitor Evaluator

Monitor Evaluators do exactly what the name suggests – monitor and evaluate the rest of the team and its ideas. They are critical thinkers, who like to take time to mull things over before coming to a considered judgment. Their feelings seldom interfere with their judgment. Monitor Evaluators show their worth in a team when it comes to making crucial decisions.

They are usually the only team members able to hold their own in a debate with a Plant, and are even capable of persuading a Plant to change her mind. They are also able to evaluate and, if necessary, challenge the enthusiastic ideas that the Resource Investigator is ably selling to the rest of the team. However, they have a tendency to be both sceptical and cynical.

## Team Worker

Team Workers' primary motivation is to work for the good of the team. Though they may be more responders than initiators, they often have a strong influence on team morale. They are the ones who are often able to defuse conflict between other team members. They foster team spirit.

Team Workers get on well with most people and are very interested in how people relate and communicate. They are encouragers of others – they help people see their strengths and handle their problems. They are always ready to support good suggestions and projects and they know how to help people pull together.

Team Workers' weaknesses are that they avoid pressured situations, and have a tendency to indecision.

## Completer

This is the last of the eight team roles, and is exactly as the name suggests. Completers ensure that the team finishes the tasks it starts, and their eye for detail means that they notice small errors and omissions.

Completers are in their element when work requires a high degree of concentration and attention. Whatever they do, they do thoroughly. They plan ahead and make sure nothing is overlooked. They have a tendency to perfectionism but are steady hard workers who enjoy being busy.

## Specialist

This ninth role has been added more recently. Specialists, as the name suggests, contribute a narrow expertise. Often single-minded, self-starting and dedicated, they bring skills in short supply.

For Specialists, true professialism is its own reward. They work simply to satisfy their own feeling of competence or widen their knowledge. They dislike taking responsibility for anything they see as outside their area of competence.

## Successful teams

The Henley research identified two types of consistently successful team. The first is the classic balanced team, in which all the roles are filled. The second is a team composed of co-operative people who love being in teams, and are flexible in the roles they adopt. Of the team roles described above, the second type of team tends to consist of Team Workers, Resource Investigators and Implementers. The problem with this type of team is a tendency to complacency, which can be offset by the introduction of a Shaper to the team.

Two other types of team can do well in certain circumstances. The first has a leader of the superstar variety. The problem with a team led by a dominant leader of this type, is that she may lead it in the wrong direction and no-one will query this. If she is right, all goes well, if not, disaster may ensue. When she leaves, the team may find it difficult to adapt to another leader after such an individualistic style of leadership.

The second type of team which is occasionally successful is a team of very intellectually talented individuals. Here the role of Coordinator is crucial, but this sort of team is often hard to manage, as it engages in destructive debate and has difficulties in decision making. This surprised the researchers, and may surprise you.

## Does your team fit the pattern?

You may be thinking, 'My team doesn't fit the successful team pattern.' We know of successful teams where not all the roles suggested for a balanced team are filled and not all the members are natural team workers. Yet they are success-ful. The model presented in this chapter may shed some light on your team situation but it is just one model, one perspec-tive. If it does fit your team, well and good; but if not, it may help you think about how your team works and about some of the roles taken up by the team members.

We have now examined the individual elements of team-work: Personality type, Gifts and abilities, Team roles.

## INDIVIDUAL ACTIVITIES

1 Try to determine what your preferred team roles are by checking the result of the Self perception inventory (Exercise 9) against the descriptions of the team roles in this chapter. Do you agree with the result you obtained on the SPI? Eg Coordinator / Monitor Evaluator (strong) with some Shaper.
2 If you are the team leader, what kind of team leader are you? Do you fit either of the leader types identified?

# TEAM ACTIVITIES

**1** Does your team fit any of the four possible successful team types? If not, is there anything you can do about this?

**2** Your team members may have clear task definitions and functions within the team. Discuss the team roles that members fulfil in addition to these. Are you making the best use of the individual attributes of your team members – ie, are they functioning in their best team roles? Do you have a balanced team? Remember that most people can take several roles.

This brings us to the end of Section 3.

# SECTION 4: OTHER ASPECTS OF TEAMWORK

## The team leader *Chapter 11*

Biblical qualifications for leadership
... Jesus our example
   ... warning to leaders
     ... followers
       ... styles of leadership
         ... gifts for leadership.

## Team management *Chapter 12*

Clear authority structure
... task definition
   ... flexibility
     ... managing change
       ... appraisal and review
         ... Moses.

## Growth and development *Chapter 13*

Good teams are effective
... personal growth
   ... teamwork develops interpersonal skills
     ... leadership team model
       ... stages of team development
         ... moving on.

## Spiritual perspectives *Chapter 14*

The relationship verses
... spiritual warfare
   ... New Testament quarrels
     ... forgiveness
       ... encouragement
         ... building a spiritual life together.

# 11

# The team leader

'The leader has a unique and crucial role in the development of any team'.[1] Possible leadership roles were discussed in the previous chapter. However, there are further aspects of leadership that we need to explore. Woodcock says that, 'In essence, the team leader's role is to ensure that the team has the right blend of roles, that skills are developed, that cooperation and support are maximised and that each individual makes his optimum contribution'[2]. Quite a tall order!

## Biblical qualifications

The Bible too is stringent in its requirements of those who aspire to leadership in the church. When Paul talks of the qualifications for leadership in 1 Timothy 3 and Titus 1, he considers two aspects – the personal qualities of the leader and the leader's family life.

Leaders should not be recent converts, but should have a good grasp of doctrinal truth. They should be honest and above reproach in all their affairs, particularly in their attitude to money. Leaders are expected to manifest the fruit of the Spirit, being gentle, self-controlled, patient and kind. If they are married, they should have stable marriages, well-run homes and disciplined children.

## Jesus, the servant leader

Jesus exemplified the major requirements for Christian leadership. First, a leader is called to be a servant. Jesus demonstrated this, even to the extent of washing the disciples' feet. He told the disciples who were jockeying for leadership positions, 'Whoever wants to become great among you must be your servant' (Mark 10:43).

Second, Jesus had the authority that comes from being filled with the Holy Spirit. He knew that authority belongs to God, and that a leader is a man under authority. He was aware that he was anointed by God and yet he knew his utter dependence on God. Everything he did, he did because the Father told him to, and he did nothing he was not told to do.

Gordon and Gail MacDonald in their book *Till the heart be touched*[3] say, 'Among the things for which Jesus will always be noted was his successful attempt at taking twelve disparate men and building a team out of them.' Jesus knew his time was limited and he left behind a trained team.

## A warning to leaders

The Lord expects more of a leader than of those who are led. The Bible teaches that there will come a day of reckoning and, if you are a leader, the Lord will hold you accountable to himself. Ezekiel 34 is a denouncement of the 'shepherds' or leaders of Israel: the Lord finds them guilty of selfishness and of leading the flock astray. He warns that he will rescue the flock by removing the shepherds.

A poor leader can cause a team real problems. Not only is there a loss of effectiveness, but poor leadership can cause distress to the team members. Obviously all leaders make mistakes. Often necessity dictates that a leader has to take more responsibility than he feels fitted for or would like.

## The cost of leadership

There are costs to be faced in leadership. It is the leader who must demonstrate the qualities necessary for a good team, such as openness and cooperation. You may not like it, you may not even be aware of it, but if you are in leadership, others will see you as a role model. Not only does the Lord expect more of you – 'Now it is required that those who have been given a trust must prove faithful' (1 Corinthians 4:2) – but other people expect more of you. This is why there is so much outrage when Christian leaders are seen to fall into sin.

Another cost to be faced in Christian leadership involves the heat of the battle. We are in a spiritual battle and leaders are more vulnerable than others because they are first in the line of fire. In times of war, the enemy always tries to destroy the leaders. Satan is no less strategic in his attacks.

## Keeping fit

If you are a leader it is important to keep yourself spiritually fit. How sad if you nurture others at your own expense or the expense of your family. Only the shepherd who constantly guards and feeds himself and his family can effectively guard and feed others.

You need the opportunity to be still and listen to God. Joyce Huggett,[4] in her writing, has done much to help those of us from the evangelical tradition to learn something of the importance of being quiet and waiting on God, as has Richard Foster[5] in his books on prayer and the disciplines of the Christian life. We do need constantly to beware of the barrenness of the busy life. Numbers 29:7 tells the Israelites that on certain days they are to 'deny yourselves and do no work'. This is very hard for some of us to follow.

## A word to followers

Your team leader needs your support and encouragement. Please do not read this chapter with a judging attitude towards your leader. Leading is not easy and we all make mistakes as we learn. We suggest below a few things that may help followers when you feel in conflict with your leader.

There is a clear biblical command to submit to those in authority (1 Peter 2:13–17). You may have to agree to differ and follow the lead given nonetheless. We are not commanded to submit only when we agree with the one in authority. God honours even imperfect leaders, and will bless you through them. As you submit to them you submit to God. John Perry[6] in Effective Christian Leadership says, 'Unless we first learn to accept the yoke of Christ and learn to be led, we can never be fit to lead.'

'How can I help my boss to succeed?' was a thought given to us in a management seminar many years ago. It is a good thought since, when you help the boss to succeed, he or she can help you to do likewise. In this way the team will succeed. Be honest with your leaders and avoid talking behind their backs. Choose a good time to confront them (not when you know they are under pressure). Try not to threaten and challenge their leadership. Tell them the things you appreciate so you do not appear totally negative.

## Type of leadership

The type of leadership required varies with the team's tasks, the stage of team development reached, and the number of people in the team. As a general rule, the larger the team the more important it is to have clearly defined leadership. Within a large team, team leadership may be the only role that the leader takes on. As a team matures, it can often function with a facilitative form of leadership, whereas it may have needed a directive form of leadership at the beginning of its formation. Even when the leadership role is facilitative and flexible, it is important that both team and leader are clear as to the role and scope of the latter.

## Styles of leadership

Leadership style varies from dominant to laid-back. For most small teams, the best type of leader is probably the democratic facilitator who would appear on a continuum thus:

Dominant ---------------------- / ------ x ------------- Laid-back

                              democratic
                              facilitator

The extremes are either dictating (making all the decisions, not allowing adequate input from others) or abdicating (giving so little leadership as to leave a vacuum), neither of which is good in any team. The democratic facilitator is like the Coordinator type in the previous chapter; the Shaper would be more directive, and appear towards the dominant end of the continuum.

## Team and working group leadership

The leadership style necessary for leading a team differs from that necessary for a working group. (The difference between teams and working groups is discussed in Chapter 2.) A team leader avoids simply interacting with those directly responsible to him, and tries instead to involve the whole team in decision making as much as possible. He does not overturn team decisions except in exceptional circumstances.

A team leader's major concern is to motivate the team so that everyone shares a common vision. He gives information openly, his role more that of colleague/friend than boss.

## Personality and leadership styles

One way of looking at leadership styles is by dividing personality into four temperaments, as Kiersey and Bates[7] do, rather than considering the sixteen personality types that Myers and Briggs postulate (Chapter 8).

A leader needs to lead his team according to his own style. He can only modify this to a certain extent, so he will nearly always lead by his preferred style. The team has to adjust to this. However, the leader can learn to understand the impact of his style on the team.

The four temperaments are, first, the intuitive thinkers (NTs), which include the ENTJ, INTJ, ENTP and INTP types; second, the intuitive feelers (NFs), which include the ENFJ, INFJ, ENFP and INFP types; third, the sensing judging types

(SJs), the ESTJ, ISTJ, ESFJ and ISFJ, and finally the sensing perceptive types (SPs), the ESTP, ISTP, ESFP and ISFP. These four temperaments produce four kinds of leader.

## The Intuitive–Thinker leader

The NT leader prefers to lead an intellectual, ideas-orientated team, such as one involved in scientific research. He loves challenges and new projects, but tends to pass on routine tasks to other team members.

The NT is a self-starter. He does not need to be told what to do or how to do it, and probably expects his team members to be self-starters too. He tends not to pay much attention to the interpersonal aspects of teambuilding and, unless the team consists of other NTs, finds it hard not to be the leader.

Under the NT leader, team meetings tend to be few, short and to the point. He is likely to sort out tasks and assign them to various team members, thus cutting down the agenda for meetings. Within the Christian world, the sort of team an NT might lead well would be the academic staff of a Bible college or other such institution.

## The Intuitive–Feeling leader

The NF often naturally comes to the forefront as a group leader or spokesperson. She is a people person and likes to develop herself and other people. Within the team, she prefers democratic decision making. She is good at encouraging other team members to participate and be involved.

However, team meetings led by an NF may be rather prolonged and tend to involve socialising, sometimes at the expense of the agenda. The NF leader could be a good leader of a church's counselling or healing ministry team.

## The Sensing–Judging leader

As a team leader, the SJ (sensing judging) person is really dependable and is fair and patient with other team members. Team meetings have a well-planned and ordered agenda.

The SJ probably functions best when a team has reached a stable stage in its development, or when its task is of the 'keeping things going' variety. He tends to be a bit resistant to change, so finds it hard to lead a 'brainstorming' team, or one that is breaking new ground. He may not find democratic, participatory decision making easy and so move towards a directive, rather than a facilitative, leadership style. He makes a good leader of an administrative team concerned with the church's finances or buildings.

## The Sensing–Perceptive leader

The SP (sensing perceptive) team leader enjoys risk-taking and changes. A naturally fraternal being, teamwork comes easily to him. He is good at troubleshooting and problem solving. He accepts and indeed expects occasional failure in himself and in others.

The SP is adept at leading a team that operates where there is action and excitement. He may be a good leader of an evangelistic outreach team, particularly if the team works in a challenging location. When a team's tasks are routine or have settled into a humdrum phase, the SP team leader may try to stir things up, simply because he's bored.

## To have or not to have a leader?

Is it necessary for a team to have a leader? Most people think it is, and probably someone always does need to be acting as the leader. However, a team can manage without the same person permanently in the leadership position. Many mature teams change their leadership to suit their circumstances.

A team of two can undoubtedly function without one designated leader. However, if you analyse your work together, you will probably become aware that one of you is actually functioning as a facilitator. Maybe one is a natural Coordinator or Shaper whose very drive assumes leadership. We find in our work together that it varies: sometimes Gordon takes the lead, sometimes Rosemary, depending on the circumstances.

We have seen small teams manage without a designated

leader. The members simply meet together and reach decisions by consensus. This seems to work better than having poor leadership with all its attendant problems.

## Gifts for leadership

Some gifts of the Holy Spirit that a leader may need include leadership, serving, teaching, pastoring, encouraging, helping and administration. If you find yourself in a position of leadership, you can ask for and expect the Lord to give you some of these gifts.

Lastly, and most importantly, a leader needs to have vision. John Perry in *Effective Christian Leadership*[8] says, 'We must have a vision for the work that God has entrusted to us. Vision is all about seeing beyond what has already been accomplished to what God has in mind for the future. Leadership without vision is doomed to mediocrity and even failure.'

# INDIVIDUAL ACTIVITIES

1 How do you measure up to the biblical standard for church leaders (1 Timothy 3 and Titus 1)?

| | |
|---|---|
| able to teach | gentle |
| not a recent convert | has a good reputation with |
| not overbearing | outsiders |
| above reproach | not quick tempered |
| sincere | temperate |
| does not pursue dishonest | tested |
| gain | keeps hold of the truth |
| children obey him | loves what is good |
| not quarrelsome | not a lover of money |
| upright and holy | disciplined |
| respectable | not given to drunkenness |
| one wife | manages own family well |
| self-controlled | hospitable |

2 How many of the attributes of Jesus' leadership do you emulate?

servanthood                    Spirit-filled
dependent on the Father     obedient
disciples others

3 Rate yourself on the leadership style continuum between dominant and laid-back. Do the team agree with this?

Dominant ------------------------- / --------------------Laid-back

4 For those in team leadership within a church – do Exercise 10, page 190.

5 Use the following to see whether your leadership style is best suited to leading a team or coordinating/running a group.

1a I consider decision making the leader's task.

1b I consider decision making for everyone together.

2a I modify decisions we have agreed when needed.

2b I abide by the decisions we have agreed, except in an emergency.

3a I involve people in solving problems only if they pertain to their area of responsibility.

3b I involve everyone in problem solving if I can.

4a My major concern is to meet current goals.

4b My major concern is to share vision and motivate the others.

5a I see goals/responsibilities as mine – the others help me.

5b I see goals/responsibilities as belonging to us all, to be achieved/faced together.

6a I share such information as each person needs to do his job.

6b I share all information openly.

If you choose more 'a' answers, then either you are leading a group or your style is more appropriate to a group. If you choose more 'b' answers, then either you are leading a team or your style is more appropriate to a team.


# TEAM ACTIVITIES

1 Each person should mark a point on the leadership style continuum which he or she feels is the right balance for

your team. Discuss this together. Is the leadership style very different from the perceived need?

2 Does the leader have time for personal needs (spiritual, emotional and physical)? Can the team help in this?

# 12

# Team management

'Unfortunately, many church leaders have not had the benefit of training in team management skills ... assistants, associates, youth workers, and others are often forced to endure depressing and non-fulfilling roles ...'

Steve Chalke[1] is saying that Christian team leaders often do not make the effort required for proper management, nor do they know how to do so. The result is that Christian teams are often poorly managed. The structure of a Christian team may make little allowance for fallen human nature. We do not like to admit to disharmony and conflict, let alone plan for them!

People have been working together for hundreds of years and systems have been set up to enable them to do so. The secular world is usually realistic about the problems inherent in teamwork. It accepts that we are sinful! Of course, this is not made explicit, but it is assumed that guidelines are necessary if people are to work together harmoniously. We can learn from secular sources about managing a team, trying to ensure that we avoid, as far as possible, treading on other people's toes when we work together.

## Clear authority structure

We have already discussed the leadership role in small teams. We now turn our attention to the team's overall authority structure.

Ambiguity about the authority structure of a team can be a major cause of friction. This is true for the team members and also for the leader. Members of the team need to be clear as to what they are responsible for, and to whom they are responsible.

There are three aspects to team authority structure:

1 Has the team a clear mandate from the group (church, company) of which it is a part? We have seen a minister take over the chairmanship of a church team because it was making decisions he did not like. He felt the members were exceeding their authority and not checking back with him. Perhaps this was because no limits had been set for them in the first place.
2 Has the leader a clearly defined mandate to lead? One small team chose a member to be the leader by default, because no-one else wanted the job. He was the least experienced, but the others did not want the administrative work the leadership role entailed – however, they didn't accept his exercise of leadership, either! They all became very frustrated.
3 Do all the members have the necessary knowledge and authority to carry out their tasks? If Jane is responsible for purchasing the AV equipment, how much can she spend? Are you leaving it to her judgment or should some limit be set?

## Clear goal and task definition

One of the first questions a team needs to ask itself is, 'What are our goals and what are the tasks we need to undertake to achieve them?' One team had been working together for some months and when asked what its goals were, the members came up with very different answers. Discussing and reaching agreement on these goals revealed why there had been some frustration in the team. The members were each aiming for a different target.

Having established team goals, the part each team member plays needs to be considered. Who is responsible for what? Each team member should be able to describe the team goals and how her tasks are contributing to these goals. She should also understand the tasks of the other team members and how the different tasks fit together. Where goals are not clearly delineated and the members' tasks are ill-defined, conflicts can easily arise. Unclear boundaries between the tasks of different team members are a common cause of misunderstanding.

## Flexibility

In the business world, job descriptions are often fairly rigid, and follow the same format throughout a national or multinational company. When interviewing to fill a job vacancy, many companies are able to be very selective, seeing lots of candidates until they find the one who most closely fits their requirements.

Christian work is often badly undermanned so we use volunteers, sometimes almost regardless of their qualifications for the task. This requires flexibility on the part of team members, since fitting the newcomer into the team may mean existing members must modify their roles. In Christian circles, in church or mission teams, it is often necessary to modify the task to fit the person. Fortunately this is sometimes easier to do than it would be in the business world.

For example, within a Bible translation team, there is technical linguistic work to carry out, a literacy programme to supervise, exegesis to do and public relations with government officials and with the local church to manage. There will also be all the practicalities of life to cope with. In a rural third world situation, these may be quite demanding! If the team consists of three or four people, there are many possible ways of dividing up these tasks. As tasks change, team members need to be flexible so that the best use is made of all their gifts.

## Conflict resolution procedures

We have already given some attention to resolving conflict, but it is not always easy to do so. Standard procedures for handling disputes, laid down ahead of time, can be of real help. There are many possible systems for allowing frustrations and difficulties to be aired. Some organisations have a regular director's time, when he is available to talk to anyone, without appointment. Pastors often have a time when they are similarly available. Members of Parliament also usually have a 'surgery' time for their constituents. All of these are set up to enable people to discuss problems, grievances or conflicts.

Sometimes the agenda item 'Any Other Business' is the opportunity for raising problems. Some job descriptions specify conflict-resolution procedures, or name an adjudicator, or ombudsman, who is not the on-line boss. Whatever system you choose, you probably need to have some procedure for allowing conflict to be aired and not buried.

## Negotiation and arbitration

When there is serious disagreement in the team which causes it to malfunction, an arbitrator is particularly necessary. We have found it useful to draw up some form of agreement, with ground rules for the continuing operation of the team. This has proved helpful with teams as diverse as married couples and large operational teams, particularly where some team members doubt that change can occur. Unless they have something in writing to which all parties have agreed, there is a tendency to refer back frequently to earlier unresolved hurts and conflicts. A negotiated settlement helps the team to move on.

# MANAGING CHANGE

Change is stressful and increases the likelihood of conflict. Particularly stressful times in a team's life occur when an individual joins an already established group, or when a team gets a new leader. When a church has a change of minister people have all kinds of expectations. Some may be hoping he will be just like the last one, while others may be hoping he will be anything but!

There are many possible ways to help defuse the tensions involved in this kind of change. One of the best is to get things out in the open and discuss them. If a new leader can make explicit his style, goals, perceived role, etc, it will help his team to accept his leadership. If he is able to delineate the differences from the previous encumbent, so much the better.

Likewise, when you join an already existing team, the more you can find out about how that team functions, the more it will help your integration into it. It is at these times of change that the kind of teambuilding presented in this book can be most helpful. Looking at the personality and gifts of the leader and the team, at your style and how each of you reacts to conflict, and talking these matters through and communicating about how you feel in the change process, will all help the team handle change better.

## Change is inevitable

Although change is stressful, it is an integral part of life, and leads to growth. A regular review time is a good opportunity to plan for change – the sort of change that is wanted and does not just happen haphazardly. Planned change is less stressful than change that takes us by surprise. Woodcook says that, 'Action planning is vital if your teambuilding efforts are to succeed.'[2] This is planning for change and involves identifying needs and considering how to meet them successfully.

## Regular appraisal and review

Appraisal is a routine part of business life. Christian teams also need times of review and appraisal. A regular review time is a good opportunity for input by team members. Their feelings, thoughts and ideas can be listened to, and acted upon. A review allows the team to learn from previous experiences and thereby to modify and improve. Even the goals of the team need regular review – they may need to be modified in line with changing circumstances and experience.

## Who should do the review?

It is possible for a team to review itself or to be reviewed by the team leader, but often it can be helpful for an outside facilitator to be brought in.

A few years ago we were preparing to lead a workshop on teamwork, specifically for single women. As part of our preparation we decided to tape-record interviews with some other single women, who were already functioning successfully in teams. We prepared a list of questions to ask them. We gave this list to the interviewees to read through before the recording session. One pair commented that just working through the questions together had been of significant help to them. They had conducted their own team review!

## Third party help

A reviewer who is not part of the team can be particularly helpful when there is no definite team leader, but can be useful in other circumstances too. One way she can review a team is by sitting in on team meetings, observing how the team functions. These observations can then be presented to the team for discussion.

Another possibility is for the reviewer to sit down with the team and ask questions. The team satisfaction questionnaire in Exercise 5 (page 173) can be given to each team member, following which they discuss the results with the reviewer. We sometimes ask each team member to give an example of where he/she is satisfied with the team and has given it a high score. This is an encouraging start. The reviewer can then ask each one to mention one item he/she has scored low. This increases mutual understanding of how each member feels about the team and will lead to discussion of some issues that may be important, but may not have been discussed. Alternatively the reviewer can simply read all the returned questionnaires and select a number of topics for discussion that are obviously of current concern.

## The team leader as reviewer

The team leader can review her own team quite effectively if she is able to be objective about it, but she may find this difficult if she is too emotionally involved. Her role is as a facilitator to help the team look at itself, its goals, methods and performance. The area she may find difficult to review is its leadership!

If the leader does oversee the review, she needs to make sure that the members are not inhibited by her presence and feel free to express dissatisfaction and suggest change. A good team will probably manage this. A team that is not at ease, in which there is no openness or honesty, will obviously find it more difficult.

## The team's environment

It is important to understand the environment in which a team operates. When reviewing team performance and looking ahead to the future it is necessary to take account of the environmental pressures that have operated in the past. It is also good to consider what they are likely to be in the future.

One team had been put together by several different entities, each suspicious of the motives of the other. Keeping these entities satisfied had taken a high toll on the team. Some members felt despondent about its future. As we helped them realise that many of the restrictions of the past would no longer apply, they could see hope for the time ahead. They could then recommit themselves to the team and its leader.

## Moses the manager

When Jethro, Moses' father-in-law, heard all that God had done in rescuing the Israelites from Egypt, he came to visit Moses in the desert. When he saw him sitting all day long settling the people's disputes, he said,

'Why do you sit alone as judge, while all these people

stand round you from morning till evening? . . . What you are doing is not good. You and these people who come to you will only wear yourselves out. The work is too heavy for you; you cannot handle it alone.'

*Exodus 18:14, 17, 18*

Jethro suggested that Moses teach the people God's laws so that they would understand for themselves the way God wanted them to live. Then he suggested Moses select capable men from among the people and appoint them as judges. He said, 'That will make your load lighter, because they will share it with you' (v22).

Moses learnt some practical things about management from Jethro. There are some good examples here: accepting outside help from secular sources; teaching people so that they understand for themselves and do not need to go for help so often; training others and delegating to them; sharing the load and taking a team approach to leadership.

We hope you have gained some practical help on the management aspects of facilitating teamwork. You may also learn from the management of teams in the corporate world.

## INDIVIDUAL ACTIVITIES

1 Are you clear as to:
   i The team's goals?
   ii Your task and its definition?
   iii Your authority to do it?
   iv What the procedure is in the event of conflict with the team or team leader?
   v How your own and the team's work is reviewed?
2 Is there opportunity for your ideas to be heard?
3 If you feel there is room for significant improvement, what can you do to bring about change?

# TEAM ACTIVITIES

1 Discussion topics.
   a) Does our team need to give more attention to the process of being a team?
   b) How does our team measure up to the following management aspects?
      i Each member has a clear task definition and knows how it fits in with the team goal(s).
      ii Each member is clear as to his/her authority and the authority of the team.
      iii If there is a difference of opinion, there is opportunity to discuss this.
      iv The team's performance and goals are regularly reviewed.
   c) Would we benefit from third party help? Do we need some training for the team or for individuals in the team?

2 Each member write a job description saying what they are responsible for and to whom.

3 Each member write their perceptions of the environment in which the team has been operating. How is it likely to change in the future? List the effects on the team. Discuss.

# 13

# Growth and development

## A good team is a seedbed for personal growth

Being part of a successful team is rewarding and enriching in itself. However, the area in which you will gain most is in your own personal growth. A good team changes all the members of that team. You will not be the same at the end of a good experience of teamwork as you were at the beginning. If you are part of a team that functions well, you will discover new things about yourself and you will increase your ability to relate to other people. You will learn to understand others better and to appreciate them more.

On the other hand, being involved in a poorly functioning team can be damaging to the individuals involved. If you are going to work as a team you may as well put effort into making it work well and thus gain the benefits that come with being part of a successful team.

## Teams are made up of individuals

A team's effectiveness is greater than that of its members individually. Nevertheless, the nature of a team reflects the characteristics of its members. As the individual members grow and develop, so the team grows and develops. If the members are stagnant in their personal development, it is unlikely that the team will grow. Therefore we need to plan for the personal growth of the team members. The growth and development of the team and that of the individual members are bound up together.

## What are we aiming at?

As we aim to be effective as individuals, so we will be effective as team members. People who are functioning well have an active approach to life. They seek challenge. They try to understand themselves and keep in touch with their own feelings. They set good standards for themselves (not unrealistically high but not below that which they are capable of achieving).

Effective people keep to their own set of personal values, while welcoming feedback and seeing constructive criticism as an opportunity for growth. They are tolerant and do not interfere with the lives of others. They are not busybodies, but have a genuine concern for other people, and are open and honest in their dealings with them.

## Training

How can individual members be helped to grow? Their growth may be largely dependent on the leader's or facilitator's encouragement or lack thereof. Individual review times can be fruitful times to explore possibilities for growth. The leader can encourage team members to take risks, try new ideas, go for challenges. Perceived weaknesses can be discussed and remedial or training options considered.

All our three children have worked at some time for large national companies which have in-house training for their staff. In the case of one company, all staff members are expected to take up at least three training options each year. If they don't do this, they are reminded at their review time of how necessary training is to ensure personal growth and development. These companies spend a lot of money on staff training. They know that it is a good investment.

## Teamwork develops our interpersonal skills

Overseas Christian workers often have to learn to work as part of a small, closely-knit team. They have to share rather cramped living quarters with colleagues. Almost all of them experience times of relationship stress, sometimes to the point where they feel like giving up and going home. We have observed that those who have been able to work through the pain of these stressful relationships have grown in the process. They have discovered things about themselves that they did not know and, perhaps, did not like. They have been able to work on these, and have learnt to appreciate others more. Like the 'living stones' of 1 Peter 2:5, they have had their corners knocked off and been able to fit together with others to become part of a 'spiritual house'.

For those of us who are married, the marriage relationship itself can be a means of growth, a means of learning to adapt to another person's idiosyncracies and to become more flexible as a result. If you live and work alone you can easily become set in your ways. This is something that is inclined to happen to all of us as we grow older. Being with other people can help to slow down the process.

## A good team develops teamwork skills

Have you noticed that the Lord uses all the experiences we go through, if we allow him? Nothing is wasted.

A young couple we know spent several years on the staff of a Christian retreat centre. Undoubtedly they learnt a lot about living and working in a team. Later, they became part of a Christian drama outreach group. This group of five young people shared a small house and lived and worked together. This was a team situation that would have tested almost anyone. Yet this team coped remarkably well. We believe this was because each individually had already developed teamwork skills.

## Interdependence

Stephen Covey,[1] describes a maturity continuum as follows –

Dependence > > > Independence > > > Interdependence

(You are responsible) (I am responsible) (We are responsible)

When we are dependent, we are expecting others to take care of us and tell us what to do. When things go wrong we blame them. When we move to independence we develop an 'I can do it', 'I am self-reliant', 'I can choose' attitude. Our Western culture has encouraged independence. In fact we have developed it so well that Peter Cappelli, an associate professor at Wharton Business School says,[2] 'It is easier to teach a sixth grader (twelve year old) about teamwork than it is to teach a college educated MBA student who has had individualism stressed by years of protracted schooling.'

To develop an attitude of interdependence requires real maturity. We need to be secure enough to let go some control of our own lives. We need to trust others, to allow the results of our work to be dependent on others and to balance a belief in our own abilities with a belief in theirs. Commenting recently on the independent attitude of many of those arriving for overseas service, one of the leaders of a small field team in a politically difficult situation said, 'We need to have a "body of Christ" mentality, with everyone a fully-functioning part – one unit working together. We can't be all "heads" and work in isolation.' Working in teams helps us develop this kind of maturity.

## Leadership team model

Most large organisations have a leadership team. If it functions well, it acts as a role model for the whole group. The leadership team – the diaconate, the eldership, the church council, or whatever the appropriate denominational name – is of vital importance in any church. A divided leadership team may leave a congregation with scars that will take years to heal. A good, united leadership team will help the congregation to move on spiritually. The team members will themselves grow through the process of being members of such a team.

Our local church tackled a large extension project. After several painful false starts, an extension executive was formed. For two or three years, the five people concerned worked very closely together, supporting each other through many difficulties. Now they can look back on this teamwork process as a significant part of their lives. It was an enriching experience for them. The whole church benefited from having the shared goal of this large practical project, which involved trusting the Lord for a great deal of money. No-one who took part will ever be the same again. Much of the success of the project was due to the extension executive working so well together. They were a good team.

# STAGES OF TEAM DEVELOPMENT

Teams develop and grow, as people do. Often we have to be patient and wait for growth and maturity in a team, just as we have to wait for growth and maturity in individuals. Your team may not be exhibiting all the signs of a good team simply because you have not had sufficient time to develop maturity. Teams may simultaneously exhibit characteristics of more than one stage in team development as they grow in some areas and not in others.

## Stage 1 Infancy: getting started

Teams usually start off with members being polite, trying to get to know each other and to gain approval. You cannot expect complete openness at this stage. Team members are afraid of 'rocking the boat' and therefore tend not to express their real feelings, nor make challenging suggestions.

In this early phase of being a team, individuals may not have learnt to listen to one another well, and may be more concerned to state their own points of view. They may also tend to be afraid to admit their weaknesses, and so miss opportunities to learn and grow.

The leader may make all the decisions – often unchallenged. Members are likely to stick to their own defined jobs, perhaps because the aims and objectives of the team have not yet been fully identified. Many teams operate at stage 1, but this is hardly real teamwork. Some term this stage *forming*.

## How to help the team move on

Engage in some 'getting to know you' activities, eg the geno-gram (Exercise 6, page 175).
Encourage openness, sharing feelings, problems etc.
Openly discuss individual strengths and weaknesses.

## Stage 2 Childhood: discovering the rules and bidding for control

As the team develops, more risks are taken in discussion, and personal feelings may be shared. Members start to listen attentively to one another and everyone begins to feel able to participate and make a contribution. Problems are discussed openly. This can lead to conflict, but, as we have already said, conflict can be good – it can lead to real understanding of one another. Quite often at this stage, the leadership or management of the team is challenged. This too can be positive, leading to change and growth. Some term this stage *storming*.

## How to help the team move on

Encourage greater frankness, allowing conflicts to surface.
Involve team members in review of team performance (see Chapter 12).
Discuss decision making and problem solving methods.
Discuss leadership styles (Chapter 11).

## Stage 3 Adolescence: moving ahead with enthusiasm and energy

At this stage, members are willing to change their preconceived ideas. They listen more carefully to each other, and absorb new facts and gain new insights. Leadership becomes more shared and democratic, less dominated by one person. At this phase of the team's life, ground rules and procedures are established for working together more methodically. Some have termed this stage *norming*.

### How to help the team move on

Encourage members to share their strengths and find a way to compensate for individual weaknesses.
Hold regular reviews.
Develop problem solving and decision making strategies.

## Stage 4 Adulthood: able to handle changing circumstances

At the mature stage, the team pulls together well. Each member is committed to team success and a high degree of group loyalty develops. Members approve of each other, and the unique contribution each makes. This does not imply total agreement on all issues, just an acceptance of differences and of each individual's validity.

The mature team is flexible, changing its strategies and even its leadership to suit circumstances. It provides an environment that fosters growth. All its members realise that continued success requires continued development. Some term this stage *performing*.

### How to help the team move on

Experiment with changes in leadership and different forms of leadership.
Encourage external assessment, review team functioning.
Encourage informal communication within the team.

### Team growth

A new member joining an existing team may well exhibit behaviour that is typical of some of the earlier stages. A team that has a changeover in membership may therefore move back to an earlier developmental stage.

Our local church leadership is an example of a team that has grown. When we first joined the church it had a congregation of just over one hundred, and the minister handled most matters. We were given a job, but soon afterwards we ground to a halt and needed to check back with the minister. He was usually so busy that it took a week or two to get an appointment. This was frustrating, and as a result, we gave our service out of a sense of duty, rather than because we felt part of a healthy team.

Eventually the church grew and, in time, other people were given specific areas of responsibility. We could go to them for help. Clear roles were established. It became a joy to work in the team, whereas previously it had been a frustrating experience.

### Teamwork is worth it

Teamwork can be rewarding for you personally, as well as help you get the job done. It may be that you grow as an individual, as does the team around you and the organisation to which you belong. We hope you will experience the many rewards as well as the obvious difficulties of being in a team.

## INDIVIDUAL ACTIVITIES

1 Does being in the team provide you with opportunities to grow? Do you have opportunities to learn new skills and try new roles?
2 Are you experiencing stress and difficulty in the team? Do you think God is allowing this? Is he causing you to grow in patience and character?
3 See if you can identify your team's developmental stage.

# TEAM ACTIVITIES

**1** Does your team plan for growth in individual members – maybe through training schemes, or members being given new and stretching tasks?

**2** A leadership team that exhibits good teamwork characteristics is a model to the rest of the organisation. Discuss this statement in relation to your team.

**3** Each team member shares something of either:

   a) how the team has caused them to grow or what they have learnt in the team, or

   b) in what way they would like the team to help them grow as individuals, eg I know I have a tendency to overlook important details. Please tell me if you think I am doing this.

**4** Identify the team's developmental stage individually and discuss your conclusions. How can the team move on to the next stage?

# *14*

# Spiritual perspectives

## The spiritual is all pervasive

Why leave the spiritual to the end of the book? Surely the spiritual is the central and vital core in any Christian team? Indeed it is, but for some people that is the problem. They feel that as Christians we should automatically be good team-workers. This can prevent them admitting weakness or failure. If we could only obey the biblical injunction to love one another all would be well! However we have to accept the fact that we will fall short of this.

You cannot avoid spiritual issues in a Christian book about teamwork. The entire Bible, the entire Christian faith, is about relationships, about living and working together, so the spiritual is an integral part of every chapter. However, we want to make explicit some things that may only have been touched on so far.

## Relationships are the key to teamwork

Our definition of a team is 'a group of people who share common objectives and who need to work together to achieve them'. When we are working we use our gifts and it is interesting that two of the most significant passages in the Bible about using our gifts, Romans 12 and 1 Corinthians 12, are followed by passages on love and on how we should live together.

Relationships are at the heart of teamwork and relationships are at the heart of the gospel. The good news is that Jesus died so that we might be reconciled to God (have our relationship restored), and be reconciled to one another. Hence the two great commandments to love God and to love each other.

The Old Testament gave rules for living together, ways to relate to God and to men. The ten commandments taught the Israelites that God does not accept the standards of the world around. Adultery, covetousness and murder are all prohibited. Jesus developed the negative 'do nots' of the Old Testament by giving us a new commandment, 'Love one another as I have loved you' (John 13:34, 15:12). When we consider his love, this seems impossible, but he will help us if we ask him.

## Relationship verses

The New Testament has a great deal to say about relationships. You may already have read the list of relationship verses from the New Testament (Exercise 1, page 160). These verses contain both positive and negative aspects of how we should treat one another. Among the positives are, 'accept one another' (Romans 15:7), 'have equal concern for each other' (1 Corinthians 12:25), 'serve one another' (Galatians 5:13), and 'be patient, bearing with one another' (Ephesians 4:2). Among the negatives are, 'do not grumble against each other' (James 5:9), 'let us not become conceited, provoking and envying each other' (Galatians 5:26) and 'stop passing judgment on one another' (Romans 14:13). These verses pose us quite a challenge.

## Spiritual warfare

We are in a battle and relationships are the battleground where Satan likes to defeat us. He will attack our relationship with God and our relationships with other people. We must guard these. He knows where we are vulnerable even if we don't. An incalculable amount of damage has been done to Christian work through Christians falling out. Splits in churches have sometimes set it back decades. Conflicts between denominations and individual churches often damage new converts and prevent people coming to faith.

Teamwork will involve us in spiritual warfare. We need to ask God to help us relate to others, to give us the grace to forgive when we cannot find the power to do so ourselves, and for his love for those we find annoying.

## So heavenly minded, no earthly use

We do not want to fall into the trap of being so heavenly minded that we are no earthly use. We're talking about real life and relationships, and not some ideal. We are flawed people who get irritable, fall out and need to forgive one another. There are very real problems involved in teamwork, and we need to face them.

We need to draw on all the spiritual resources we can: asking the Holy Spirit to help us; reading and applying the Word of God; praying about the team, and yet, at the same time, we need to be down-to-earth and realistic. If we are not careful, we can hide behind a kind of misplaced spirituality, unable to express what we really feel because it means facing the fact that we fall short. If we think Christians should not feel angry, frustrated, even jealous of others, we deny the problems we face and lose the opportunity to solve them. We can even end up being dishonest, in that we deny the reality of the situation. The Christian faith, which should be the springboard to good relationships, can be used to hide the truth from ourselves, and even to manipulate others. 'God has called me to do this' can mean 'I want to do it'. By using this phrase, I put myself above argument. I don't want to listen to anyone else's point of view.

## New Testament quarrels

Although we may try to hide our disagreements or call them by another name, the Bible is open and honest about the disagreements that occurred between believers. James and John, both members of Jesus' team, wanted recognition and power (Mark 10:35–45). When the other disciples heard about this, they became indignant. They argued about status.

It is not a very edifying story but one which is true to life. People frequently do seek both power and recognition, and arouse jealousy in others if they obtain these.

Paul and Barnabas had 'such a sharp disagreement that they parted company' (Acts 15:39). This was over a matter of principle and reflected the very different temperaments of the two men concerned. There are still conflicts in Christian teams between strong-minded people over matters of principle on which they differ. If we accept that when Christian men and women work closely together they will sometimes fall out, we are being realistic. Accepting the inevitability of conflict helps us to handle and deal with it when it occurs.

## Forgiveness

Forgiveness is not an optional extra for Christians. It is essential if we want to receive the Lord's forgiveness. 'For if you forgive men when they sin against you, your heavenly Father will also forgive you. But if you do not forgive men their sins, your Father will not forgive your sins' (Matthew 6:13, 14).

Jesus emphasised his point by telling a story – the parable of the unmerciful servant. In this story, the servant, who has been forgiven the debt of an enormous amount of money, will not forgive the much lesser debt of a fellow servant. When the master finds out, he withdraws his forgiveness of the original servant and has him tortured. Jesus said that that is how our heavenly Father will treat us if we do not forgive (Matthew 18:21–35). This is strong stuff! I'm not sure how much we really believe it. If we did, we'd be very quick to get rid of all our grudges.

The more closely we relate with others, the more opportunity we have to offend and be offended. As we work in a team, we will hurt each other. How vital it is that we give and receive forgiveness. You are fallible too, for you have weaknesses and shortcomings and you need to be forgiven.

## It can be done

There are some tremendous examples of forgiveness in the lives of well-known Christians. Corrie ten Boom,[1] who was held by the Nazis in Ravensbrück, where her sister died, was speaking on forgiveness in post-war Germany. One of the Ravensbrück guards was in the meeting, having become a Christian. When he asked her for forgiveness, she had a struggle. She said to forgive him was the most difficult thing she had ever had to do.

> 'For I had to do it – I knew that. The message that God forgives has a prior condition: that we forgive those who have injured us... I knew it not only as a commandment of God, but as a daily experience. Since the end of the war I had had a home in Holland for victims of Nazi brutality. Those who were able to forgive their former enemies were able also to return to the outside world and rebuild their lives, no matter what the physical scars. Those who nursed their bitterness remained invalids. It was as simple and as horrible as that.'

Corrie forgave that man by an act of the will.

> 'For a long moment we grasped each other's hands, the former guard and the former prisoner. I had never known God's love so intensely as I did then. But even so, I realised it was not my love. I had tried, and did not have the power. It was the power of the Holy Spirit as recorded in Romans 5:5, "Because the love of God is shed abroad in our hearts by the Holy Ghost which is given unto us".'

More recently, Gordon Wilson's daughter was killed by an IRA bomb blast at Enniskillen in Northern Ireland. He is a Christian and he publicly forgave the bombers.

## A servant attitude

In the chapter on team leadership, we discussed Jesus' example of a team leader who had the attitude of a servant. However, it is not just the leader who is called to have that attitude. We are all to 'submit to one another' (Ephesians 5:21) and to 'serve one another in love' (Galatians 5:13). None of us likes taking the servant role. Our pride and our selfishness fight hard against it, and make us want to suit ourselves and put ourselves first.

## Encouragement

Surely one thing that should mark a Christian team is that the members encourage one another. We all need encouragement. When we receive it, we blossom and are able to produce our best work. We are actually told to 'encourage one another daily' (Hebrews 3:13). Perhaps we really do need encouragement that often! Most of us are only too aware of our own weaknesses, faults and shortcomings. We are all insecure to some extent and we need to hear other people tell us we're OK. When we give encouragement to others, it can help us not to be critical of them, but rather to look for their good qualities.

## The Bible speaks to groups

Much of the New Testament is addressed to the body of Christ rather than to individuals. Coming from our Western, strongly individualistic society, we often interpret it individually. The biblical cultures were strongly corporate, and the scriptures assume a greater measure of interdependence than we are used to. The Old Testament lifestyle was a communal one – in many ways like that of a rural community in the third world today. A team takes on board the idea of corporate responsibility. It is not enough for each of us to feel that we are only responsible for our own life.

When Achan took some of the devoted things the whole nation suffered defeat at Ai (Joshua 7). Everyone was affected by one individual's sin. When one man, Noah, was righteous, his entire extended family was saved. There are numerous such examples. Sin by one member of the team can sour the whole group. God is interested in our attitudes as a team. We may need to look at the Bible again and let it speak to us as a team.

## Building and maintaining a spiritual life together

It has been said that the family that prays together stays together. We can add that the team that prays together is much more likely to stay together and to be an effective team.

Prayer so easily gets crowded out. Time pressure seems to mitigate against fellowship. There is always so much to be done. Problems in relationships often cause our fellowship to be shallow and unreal. Fellowship times can become meaningless, lacking in truth and openness. Individual personal problems also cause our fellowship times to suffer. Where our own spiritual life is in the doldrums, we have nothing to share or to give to others. Tiredness, sickness, staleness can all prevent us enjoying Christian fellowship together.

## What can we do to maintain fellowship?

This depends on the type of team. A married couple team would be well advised to pray together every day. Other teams – the worship team or choir, the youth team, the leadership team – need to pray together regularly. Prayer times should include an opportunity for sharing and praying for each other's personal needs and difficulties, as well as prayer for the work.

Our fellowship with God and our fellowship one with another are both vital to the success of our Christian teams. Jesus in his prayer for all believers prayed, 'that all of them may be one, Father, just as you are in me and I am in you' (John 17:21).

We have now examined the 'other aspects' of the team-building model: The team leader, Team management, Growth and development, Spiritual perspectives.

# INDIVIDUAL ACTIVITIES

1 Pray for each member of your team and ask for the Lord's direction in all that you do together.
2 Read the relationship verses in Exercise 1 (page 160) and ask the Lord to speak to you about your responsibility to other members of the team.
3 Is there anyone on the team whom you need to forgive, or from whom you need to ask forgiveness?

# TEAM ACTIVITIES

1 Each member tell the others which of the activities from the relationship verses are already being practised in the team. Which ones are missing? Eg I feel we do serve one another and we don't grumble against one another.
I would like encouragement to be practised more because I get discouraged easily and need others to tell me they appreciate my efforts.
2 Does God always expect us to work closely with other people? Has our independent Western culture caused us to apply the Bible to ourselves individually when God is speaking to his people communally?
3 Each one share a particular need and pray for one another about these.

This brings us to the end of Section 4.

# 15

# Building your team profile

It is all too easy to read a book, think 'That's helpful', then forget all about it and do nothing. For this reason, we suggest you write something down – a team profile. You should be able to use it in the days, weeks and months to come, to help make your teamwork more effective. We also hope you have done some of the individual exercises, and perhaps the group exercises together.

## What is a team profile?

A team profile may be built up through taking a series of snapshots of the team from different angles, eg, getting a clear picture of the aims of the team, what you each mean by commitment, how the team is managed and what weaknesses there are which need attention. Building a team profile from the exercises you have done together is one possible way of doing a team review. The profile can also incorporate a kind of agreement or contract for the team.

## Model of teamwork

Look back at the model for teamwork that we have been following. We started in chapters one to three with why teamwork is important to Christians, and what makes good or bad teams.

The next four chapters were about the four interpersonal aspects of teamwork – Expectations/Assumptions; Commitment; Communication; Conflict Resolution.

The following three chapters moved on to what each individual brings to the team – Your personality; Your Gifts and Abilities; Your Team Roles.

Next, some management aspects of teamwork were outlined to give a structure that can help us work together – The Team Leader; Team Management; Growth and Development.

Finally came Spiritual Perspectives of teamwork, considering what God has to say on the subject.

## Writing an individual profile

A team profile can be an amalgamation of the individual profiles of each of its members. You can compile an individual profile by working through each chapter and making notes on what you could do to improve your part in the team. You, on your own, can significantly alter your team for good.

## A SAMPLE INDIVIDUAL PROFILE

*Teamwork concepts* (Chapters 1–3) – Our youth leaders' team is not functioning well and we would benefit from some teambulding. I will bring it up at the next meeting.

*Expectations/assumptions* (Chapter 4) – My poor relationship with Harry could be linked to my feelings about my father. I will discuss this with the pastor.

*Commitment* (Chapter 5) – I have taken on too much and am not giving adequate commitment to the team. I need to find out what God wants me to do about this, what I should prune from my life.

*Communication* (Chapter 6) – I do not always communicate clearly. I will listen to my team mates more carefully and try to express myself more succinctly.

*Conflict resolution* (Chapter 7) – My style is . . . So and so's style is . . . We clash because . . . I will try to . . .

### Writing a team profile

To build a team profile together, discuss each of the aspects of teamwork, using the results of both your individual activities and the group activities.

## A SAMPLE TEAM PROFILE

The following is a sample team profile of an imaginary team. There is the minister, David, who came to the church only a year ago, and the assistant minister, Peter, who has been there for two years. Other members are Tom, Philip and Jenny, who have all been on the team for several years, and John and Pat who joined it three months ago after their election at the annual church meeting.

David, as the 'ex officio' leader, asked each person to read through this book and to write their own profile. They met together for a review day and compiled the following team profile review.

## TEAM PROFILE – PODSWORTH CHURCH ELDERS' TEAM

### 1 Teamwork concepts (Chapters 1–3)

We have agreed that it is important to spend time on the process of building ourselves into an effective team. Therefore, we should not spend all our time together doing business and neglect our relationships with each other.

Thankfully, we do exhibit some of the signs of a good team! But we also have some of the symptoms of a poor one. A few members have been feeling frustrated because they do not always know what is happening. This is probably because a lot of team business is done informally and verbally. John and Pat still feel like outsiders. The others need to help them feel that they belong. This initial discussion of our team has encouraged us to go ahead with a complete team review using the other chapters of the book.

## 2 Expectations and assumptions (Chapter 4)

We now realise how different we are. Three of us come from another denominational background, and thus bring different expectations and assumptions. We need to work on understanding each others' background assumptions.

One member, John, was converted as an adult five years ago. All the others come from Christian family backgrounds. John has a perspective the rest of us lack, in that he can empathise more easily with the people we are trying to reach. We have asked him to think through how we might effectively communicate with local people.

## 3 Commitment (Chapter 5)

There was some discussion about the level of commitment elders should have to the team. We all consider that being part of the elders' team is our most important church commitment. For this reason we agreed:

   i  David (the minister) needs more administrative help so that he has time to prepare for meetings and is more able to involve the team in important decisions.

  ii  Tom and John need to be released from some of their other church responsibilities to enable them to give a realistic commitment to the elders' team.

 iii  Commitment to the team involves loyalty to each other, regular prayer and support for each other.

## 4 Communication (Chapter 6)

There have been a few cases of miscommunication and lack of communication in the team. These arise particularly when decisions are made outside formal meetings, eg by phone, after church, etc. These decisions will now be reported to the other team members, either by means of a short memo or verbally at the next meeting. Two members tend to miscommunicate on a personal level – they are going to discuss how they can communicate better with each other. If necessary, they will ask for third party help with this.

## 5 Conflict (Chapter 7)

We like to have a feeling of harmony in the group, and do not really allow for conflict. For this reason important issues sometimes get 'swept under the carpet', causing problems later. We need to learn to disagree sometimes. Some conflict could be good for us. We will encourage all members to voice their concerns, particularly those who are less vocal. We need everyone's input. Alternative points of view will be acceptable!

Although there has not been much open conflict, some members were badly hurt by a majority decision we took to extend the church hall. Apology has now been made, and forgiveness given and received. We are aiming for a spirit of unity, by being more open with one another, and working through our disagreements rather than hiding or running away from them.

## 6 Personality type (Chapter 8)

Using the Myers Briggs personality model, we realise that our team is fairly evenly balanced in terms of making judgments (the feeling – thinking continuum). However we have almost no intuitives and are heavily weighted with sensers. We have not made enough use of intuitives in the congregation in leadership roles and need to consider how we can rectify this. We need the 'visionary' emphasis intuitives could bring to our team.

## 7 Gifts and abilities (Chapter 9)

This chapter has implications for the wider church membership. We want to make sure that all members of the congregation are able to use their gifts to the full in the church's life. We will begin a teaching series on gifts and start with 'God's rules for using our gifts'.

## 8 Team roles (Chapter 10)

David – Shaper
Peter – Implementer/Completer
Tom – Resource Investigator/Plant
Philip – Monitor Evaluator
Jenny – Team Worker/Implementer
John – Team Worker/Completer
Pat – Coordinator/Team Worker

David is the leader of the church and, as a Shaper, takes the decisions of the elders' team and implements them in the church. At the moment we are functioning more like a working group than a team, but want to move toward a shared leadership team approach. Pat could set up and lead a group doing outreach. We need to encourage Tom to share his ideas more.

## 9 The team leader (Chapter 11)

We all agree that the leadership style we prefer is somewhere between dominant and laid-back. David's natural style is towards the dominant end but he wants to involve the team more in decision making and hopes to do this as it gains in experience. David's natural style is similar to that of a Sensing–Judging leader.

## 10 Team management (Chapter 12)

We feel this aspect of the team is working fairly well. We have several people with managerial experience. Most of us are organised individuals, and we make an organised team.

## 11 Growth and development (Chapter 13)

Are members of the team growing as individuals? Is the team a good environment in which to grow? We haven't discussed this fully as yet. There could be important implications for us.

Are we a good teamwork model for the rest of the church?

As we work to improve our teamwork, we hope that this will encourage the rest of the church and other teams in it.

## 12 Spiritual perspectives (Chapter 14)

We want the elders' team to work together in a way that models the New Testament pattern – we will make sure particularly that we allow time for maintaining fellowship within the team. In addition to business meetings we have agreed to meet for a 'prayer breakfast' at 8 am each Saturday. This is specifically to share fellowship, pray for one another and deal with any matters that could cause a break in fellowship or damage relationships within the team.

## Conclusion

Some important issues have arisen from this team review. It is recommended that we have a whole session discussing these issues to help us to improve our teamwork. We also recommend a review day each year to assess our team performance and progress. A full teambuilding weekend workshop every other year would also be useful.

*Elders' Team Review Committee*

## The promised land?

What is the prognosis for your team? Is it going to be a desert experience for the members or are you going on to the good things God has for you as a team? Are you going to press on to the milk and honey of good living and working relationships? Jesus' team went on to change the world.

# References

Books marked * are listed more fully on pages 156 to 159.

## Chapter 2 Living and working with others

1 'Coals to Newcastle', Keith Wheatley, *Sunday Times Business World* supplement, 30 March 1991.
2 Massachusetts Institute of Technology, J D Power and Associates.

## Chapter 3 What is a good team?

1 M Woodcock, *Team Development Manual*.*

## Chapter 4 Expectations and assumptions

1 J Huggett, *Conflict: Friend or Foe?* p 48.*

## Chapter 5 Commitment – the essence of a team

1 'The Discipline of Teams', Katzenbach and Smith, *Harvard Business Review*, March–April 1993.

## Chapter 6 Communication – oiling the parts

1 G and R Jones, *Naturally Gifted*, pp 176–179.*

## Chapter 7 Conflict is inevitable

1 P Bell and P Jordan, *Conflict*, p 139.*

## Chapter 8 Personality type

1 Kiersey and Bates, *Please Understand Me.**
2 Grant, Thompson, Clark, *From Image to Likeness.**

## Chapter 9 Gifts and abilities

1 G and R Jones, *Naturally Gifted*, p v.*
2 G and R Jones, *Naturally Gifted*, p 132.*

## Chapter 11 The team leader

1 Woodcock, *Team Development Manual*, p 31.*
2 Woodcock, *Team Development Manual*, p 33.*
3 Gordon and Gail MacDonald, *Till the Heart be Touched*, Highland Books, Guildford, 1992.
4 Joyce Huggett, *Listening to God*, Hodder & Stoughton, 1986.
5 Richard Foster, *The Celebration of Discipline* and *Prayer*, Hodder & Stoughton, London, 1989 and 1992.
6 J Perry, *Effective Christian Leadership*, p 18.*
7 Kiersey and Bates, *Please Understand Me*, section V, p 129.*
8 J Perry, *Effective Christian Leadership*, p 98.*

## Chapter 12 Team management

1 'Managing Your Team', Steve Chalke, *Alpha*, November 1992.
2 Woodcock, *Team Management Manual*, p 38.*

## Chapter 13 Growth and development

1 Steven Covey, *The Seven Habits of Highly Effective People*, Simon and Schuster, New York, 1989.
2 Andrew Erdman, *Fortune* magazine, 10 August 1992.

# Chapter 14 Spiritual perspectives

1 Corrie ten Boom and Jamie Buckingham, *Tramp for the Lord*, Hodder & Stoughton, London, 1976, p 52.

# Resources

1 *Naturally Gifted*, Gordon and Rosemary Jones, Scripture Union, London, 1991. (Also published in the USA – *Naturally Gifted: A Self-Discovery Workbook*, IVP, Illinois.) This book provides tools to help you discover your natural gifts. A range of tests on interests, aptitudes, values, temperament, etc, form the core of the book. Set in the context of a biblical look at individuality, it will help you understand yourself and your gifts and therefore the contribution you can make to a team.

2 *Gifts Differing*, Isobel Briggs Myers, Consulting Psychologists Press, California, USA, 1980. Explains the work of Myers and Briggs on personality type leading to the development of the Myers Briggs Type Indicator.

3 *Introduction to Type in Organisational Settings*, Sandra Hirsh and Jean Kummerow, Consulting Psychologists Press, California, USA, 1987. This book helps the reader to understand the use of the MBTI in organisational settings. It shows the contributions to the organisation, leadership style, preferred work environment, and potential pitfalls for each of the sixteen personality types.

4 *Please Understand Me*, Kiersey and Bates, Prometheus Nemesis Book Company, California, USA, 1978. An easy to read book explaining temperament type in relation to Jung and in relation to Myers Briggs. Applies temperament theory to mating, parenting and leadership styles. Contains a self-administered temperament sorter yielding an MBTI type result.

5 *Working Together: A Personality Centred Approach to*

*Management*, Isachsen and Berens, Neworld Management Press, California, USA, 1980. The authors have used the MBTI as a management tool in helping people to work together. The book lists the characteristics and implications of the management style, values, attitudes, skills, driving force, energy direction, authority, orientation, conflict style, learning style and blind spots/pitfalls for each of the sixteen types.

6 *God's Diverse People*, Lawrence and Diana Osborn, Daybreak, Darton, Longman and Todd Ltd, London, 1991. The British authors link personality type with Christian living. There are chapters on prayer, communication and Christian leadership.

7 *Myers Briggs Type Indicator*, Katherine Briggs and Isobel Myers, Consulting Psychologists Press, California, USA, 1976. This indicator is only available to those trained in its use. Oxford Psychologists Press sell it in the UK.

8 Courses in the UK on the use and interpretation of the MBTI are available from, among others:

Bradford Diocesan House, Parceval Hall, Appletreewick, Skipton, North Yorkshire BD23 6DG.

Emmaus House, Diocesan Pastoral and Retreat Centre, Clifton Hill, Bristol, Avon BS8 4PD.

Crusade for World Revival, Waverley Abbey House, Waverley Lane, Farnham, Surrey GU9 8EP.

*Vision* magazine, available from National Retreat Centre, Liddon House, 24 South Audley Street, London W1Y 5DL, lists other MBTI course providers.

9 *Team Spirit: People working with People*, David Cormack, MARC, an imprint of Kingsway Publications Ltd, Eastbourne, 1973. Dr Cormack considers the risks and rewards of teambuilding, styles of leadership, criticism and encouragement, the use and abuse of authority and conflict and reconciliation.

10 *Peacing Together: From Conflict to Resolution*, David Cormack, MARC, an imprint of Monarch Publications, Eastbourne, 1989. A comprehensive look at conflict, working through the meaning, practice, barriers, risks and the price of reconciliation.

11 *Team Development Manual* (second edition), Mike

Woodcock, Gower Publishing Co, Aldershot, 1989. It is unusual to find such a comprehensive and technically competent book that is to easy to read. Contains basic teambuilding theory, the building blocks of teamwork and a good resource section for those who want to read and study further.

12 *50 Activities for Teambuilding*, Mike Woodcock, Gower Publishing Co, Aldershot, 1989. These activities for teambuilding workshops have clear goals and are linked to specific teamwork problems.

13 *Conflict: Handling Conflict in the Local Church*, Pauline Bell and Pauline Jordan, Scripture Union, London, 1992. Shows the damage caused to the local church and its members by unresolved conflict. Presents case histories and explores some of the contributing factors to the conflict, together with some suggestions for handling conflict in the local church more effectively.

14 *Conflict: Friend or Foe?* Joyce Huggett, Kingsway Publications, Eastbourne, 1984. The situations addressed include friendship, family life, marriage and the church. Friction and conflict are inevitable in these situations and the author suggests how to handle and even benefit from them.

15 *Effective Christian Leadership*, John Perry, Hodder & Stoughton, London, 1983. A comprehensive, easy to read book considering the responsibility, cost and scope of Christian leadership.

16 *Management Teams: Why They Succeed or Fail*, R Meredith Belbin, Heinemann Professional Publishing Ltd, Oxford, 1981. This book sets out the findings of Dr Belbin's research in conjunction with Henley Management College, giving indicators of how to predict winning teams and unsuccessful teams from the personality make-up of the team members.

17 *Team Roles at Work*, R Meredith Belbin, Butterworth-Heinemann Ltd, Oxford, 1993. Dr Belbin develops his ideas on team roles further, using feedback gained through users of his work.

18 *Leading Groups*, Margaret Parker, Epworth Press, London, 1987. Aimed specifically at helping those leading small groups in the local church. A very practical book with plenty of workable suggestions.

**19** *Team Building: An exercise in leadership*, Robert Maddux, Kogan Page Ltd, London, 1989. (Crisp Publications Inc, 1986, in US.) A short workbook, 77pp, with particular emphasis on helping the leader to build a team.

**20** *Caring Enough to Forgive*, David Augsberger, Regal Books, California, USA, 1981. A comprehensive look at forgiveness including false forgiveness, which can distort or even deny the truth of the situation (see also 21 below).

**21** *Caring Enough to Confront*, David Augsberger, Herald Press, Pennsylvania, USA, 1975.

**22** *Making Vocational Choices: A Theory of Careers*, John Holland, Prentice-Hall, New Jersey, USA, 1973. John Holland's theory of careers showing vocational environments and linking these with personality types.

**23** *Understanding How Others Misunderstand You*, Voges and Braund, Moody Press, Chicago, USA, 1990. Another personality parameter that has proved helpful in understanding interpersonal relationships. Particularly popular in Christian circles.

**24** *Till the Heart be Touched*, Gordon and Gail MacDonald, Highland Books (of IPS Ltd), Guildford, 1992. How to build intimacy in close relationships.

**25** *Leader Effective Training*, Thomas Gordon, Bantam Books Inc, New York, USA, 1977. This book covers many aspects of teambuilding from the perspective of the team leader trying to improve teamwork.

**26** *Learning to Love People You Don't Like*, Floyd McClung, Kingsway Publications, Eastbourne, 1987 (First published as, *Father Make Us One*). A very practical book giving steps on how to bring harmony and reconciliation to Christian relationships.

# Exercise 1

## RELATIONSHIP VERSES

A list of scriptural verses that refer to relationships, which may be used at any point in the teambuilding process.

1 'Be at peace with each other' Mark 9:50.
2 'Wash one another's feet' (a servant attitude) John 13:14.
3 'Love one another' John 13:34.
4 'Each member belongs to all the others' Romans 12:5.
5 'Be devoted to one another' Romans 12:10.
6 'Honour one another above yourselves' Romans 12:10.
7 'Rejoice with those who rejoice; mourn with those who mourn' (empathise) Romans 12:15.
8 'Live in harmony with one another' Romans 12:16.
9 'Stop passing judgment on one another' Romans 14:13.
10 'Let us therefore make every effort to do what leads to peace and to mutual edification' Romans 14:19.
11 'Accept one another' Romans 15:7.
12 'Instruct one another' Romans 15:14.
13 'Greet one another' Romans 16:16.
14 [Do not take] 'pride over against another' 1 Corinthians 4:6.
15 'Wait for each other' (be considerate) 1 Corinthians 11:33.
16 'Have equal concern for each other' 1 Corinthians 12:25.
17 'Serve one another' Galatians 5:13.

18 'If you keep on biting and devouring each other, watch out or you will be destroyed by each other' Galatians 5:15.

19 'Let us not become conceited, provoking and envying each other' Galatians 5:26.

20 'Carry each other's burdens' Galatians 6:2.

21 'Let us do good to all people, especially to those who belong to the family of believers' Galatians 6:10.

22 'Consider others better than yourselves' Philippians 2:3.

23 'Be kind and compassionate to one another' Ephesians 4:32.

24 'Be patient, bearing with one another' Ephesians 4:2.

25 'Submit to one another' Ephesians 5:21.

26 'Each of you should look not only to your own interests, but also to the interests of others' Philippians 2:4.

27 'Do not lie to each other' (be honest) Colossians 3:9.

28 'Forgive whatever grievances you may have against one another' Colossians 3:13.

29 'Teach and admonish one another with all wisdom' Colossians 3:16.

30 'Build each other up' 1 Thessalonians 5:11.

31 'Make sure that nobody pays back wrong for wrong, but always try to be kind to one another' 1 Thessalonians 5:13.

32 'Encourage one another daily' Hebrews 3:13.

33 'Spur one another on towards love and good deeds' Hebrews 10:24.

34 'Do not slander one another' James 4:11.

35 'Do not grumble against each other' James 5:9.

36 'Confess your sins to each other' James 5:16.

37 'Pray for each other' James 5:16.

38 'Offer hospitality to one another without grumbling' 1 Peter 4:9.

39 'Each should use whatever gift he has to serve others, faithfully administering God's grace' 1 Peter 4:10.

40 'Clothe yourselves with humility toward one another' 1 Peter 5:5.

41 'Have fellowship one with another' 1 John 1:7.

## Individually

**1** Make a note of those verses you feel you need to apply personally.

**2** Meditate on one verse each day, allowing the Lord to speak to you and to help you apply these verses to your relationships.

## As a team

**1** Each of you note three verses that you feel would be of particular help to the team. Discuss your findings together.

**2** List the nouns that describe good relationships.

   eg Honesty – Colossians 3:9
       Commitment – Romans 12:5
       Peace – Mark 9:50
       Servant Attitude – John 13:14
       Acceptance – Romans 15:7

Now rate the team out of ten for each of these. Discuss together.

# Exercise 2

## THE ZIN OBELISK GAME

This game could be played appropriately as part of a team-building activity linked to Chapters 1, 2, 6, 7 or 11. Its purpose is to study the process of information sharing in teams, and leadership, cooperation and conflict issues.

### Method

1 The facilitator distributes the group instruction sheet below, one to each member of the team.
2 The information cards are divided *randomly* among the team members.
3 The team completes the task.
4 The facilitator leads a review of the experience using the review sheet and, if necessary, the answer and rationale sheet.
5 Approximately twenty-five minutes is required to complete the activity, with additional time for review.
6 Teams of five to eight players may take part.

### Notes and variations

1 Players may complete review sheets individually before the group process takes place.
2 Extra irrelevant information may be introduced to compli-

cate the task.

3 Process observers may be used.

## Group instruction sheet

In the ancient city of Atlantis a solid, rectangular obelisk called a Zin was built in honour of the Goddess Tina. The structure took less than two weeks to complete and your task is to determine on which day of the week it was completed. You may share the information you have on the cards but you may not show the cards to other players.

## Information cards

Cards measuring approximately 50 mm × 75 mm should be prepared each featuring one of the following sentences:

The basic measurement of time in Atlantis is a day.

An Atlantian day is divided into Schlibs and Ponks.

The length of the Zin is 10 metres.

The height of the Zin is 30 metres.

The depth of the Zin is 5 metres.

The Zin is built of stone blocks.

Each block is 30 cubic decimetres.

A decimetre is one-tenth of a metre.

Day 1 in the Atlantian week is Aquaday.

Day 2 in the Atlantian week is called Neptiminus.

Day 3 in the Atlantian week is called Sharkday.

Day 4 in the Atlantian week is called Mermaidday.

Day 5 in the Atlantian week is called Daydoldrum.

There are 5 days in the Atlantian week.

The working day has 9 Schlibs.

Each worker takes rest periods during the working day totalling 16 Ponks.

There are 8 Ponks in a Schlib.

Workers each lay 150 blocks per Schlib.

At any time when work is taking place there is a gang of 9 people on site.

One member of each gang has religious duties and does not lay blocks.

No work takes place on Daydoldrum.
What is a Cubitt?
A Cubitt is a cube, all sides of which measure 1 Megalithic Yard.
One metre equals a Megalithic Yard.
Does work take place on Sunday?
What is a Zin?
Which way up does the Zin stand?
The Zin is made of green blocks.
Green has a spcial religious significance on Mermaidday.
Each gang includes two women.
Work starts on the first day of the Atlantian week.
Only one gang is working on the construction of the Zin.

## Review sheet

1 What actions helped the group accomplish the task?
2 Which actions hindered the group in completing the task?
3 How did leadership emerge in the team?
4 Who participated most?
5 Who participated least?
6 What feelings did you experience as the task progressed?
7 What suggestions would you make to improve team performance?

## Answer and rationale sheet

The answer is Neptiminus.

## Rationale

1 The dimensions of the Zin mean that it contains 1500 cubic metres of material.
2 Blocks are 30 cubic decimetres each, therefore 50,000 blocks are required.
3 There are 7 working Schlibs in a day.
4 Each worker lays 150 blocks per Schlib, therefore each worker lays 1050 blocks per day.
5 There are 8 workers per day meaning that 8,400 blocks

are laid per working day.

6 The 50,000th block is therefore laid on the sixth working day.

7 As work does not take place on Daydoldrum the sixth working day is Neptiminus.

Reproduced with permission from *50 Activities for Teambuilding*, Mike Woodcock, Gower, Aldershot, 1988.

# Exercise 3

## TRIVIAL PURSUIT TEAM EXERCISE

Trivial Pursuit is a popular game that is usually played by people individually. It can also be played in teams and used as a tool to learn more about teamwork. It shows that teamwork pays, and demonstrates decision making by consensus. This exercise could be used with Chapter 2.

### Instructions

Divide into two teams.

Team 1: Discuss each question and come to consensus on the answer before giving it.

Team 2: Simply ask each other who knows the answer and 'vote' on the most likely one without discussing it.

When you have finished one round, reverse the roles. All things being equal, the team that co-operates and reaches consensus should get the best results.

Let's give an actual example of using consensus, one in which we were involved. There was a question giving the names of three ports and asking which country they were in. The team looked completely nonplussed. They had no idea. Someone suggested somewhere in the Far East. Then one member said, 'Isn't "porto" Portuguese?' Another member asked which countries have Portuguese as their national language. Slowly, by using all the small bits of information which different members had, we arrived at the correct solution, which was Brazil.

# Exercise 4

## THINGS TO TALK ABOUT

The following list of topics was developed to help those about to form a Bible translation team, and could be useful whenever teamwork involves members living in close quarters. It could be used with Chapters 1 and 2, and covers some of the topics developed further in later chapters.

Perhaps you are going to share a flat with members of a team to which you belong and know that if you do not get on together it will be a big strain on all of you; or perhaps you and others are going to form an evangelistic team and go to Eastern Europe where you will have to live and work closely together. Chatting over the following issues should help you determine if you could make either of these things work.

## 1 Finances

- how much of an issue are finances likely to be?
- to what extent shall we have a common purse?
- who will pay for what?
- do you like to spend or to conserve?
- do you tend to spend on big items or small items – on food/clothing/work/holidays/recreation/other?

## 2 Food

- what kinds of food do you like?
- how important is food to you?
- what is your attitude to diet? (important to eat right foods versus can't stand food fads).
- what is your attitude to food that is unfamiliar to you?
- who prepares/who cleans up?
- entertaining – who and how often?

## 3 Cleanliness/tidiness

- tidiness ... house ... bedroom ... office
- hygiene ... food ... dishes ... water ... (I only drink bottled water!)

## 4 Privacy/Ownership

- when, where and how firmly closed is the door?
- do you need to ask to use my things?

## 5 Relationships with others

- lots of non-mutual friends versus expecting to share most friends together?

## 6 Work roles and responsibilities

- do you expect very separate roles?
- do you expect to work closely together?

## 7 Perfectionism

- if a job is worth doing is it worth doing properly?
- as long as it works who cares?
- slow perfectionist versus quick and slipshod?

## 8 Control or power

- who leads?
- what does the less dominant person want?

## 9 Time

– how important is timekeeping?
– how important is it to plan ahead?
– do you like to keep to schedule?

## 10 Competition

– are we likely to compete with each other?
– how will I feel when the other person is much better than I am at some things?

## 11 Strengths and weaknesses

– what strengths do I bring to the team?
– what weaknesses do I bring to the team?

## 12 Negative feelings

– how do you react when you are angry?
– do you have mood swings?
– what upsets you most?

## 13 Mutual support and encouragement

– how can we be a support to each other?
– how do I signal I need help?
– what helps when I am down?
– how do I react to stress? (run, keep up appearances, fall apart!)
– what stresses me most?

## 14 Devotional times

– will we have times of praying together ... how often and when?
– what sort of items for prayer shall we share (work/ personal)?
– will we share how we feel, what the Lord is saying to us?

## 15 Decisions

- how do I make them (facts versus feelings ... gut level versus careful analysis)?

## 16 Commitment

- how much commitment do I expect from the other(s)?
- to each other, to the project?

# Exercise 5

## TEAM SATISFACTION QUESTIONNAIRE

This questionnaire is designed to measure the degree of satisfaction you are experiencing in the team. It could be a useful exercise to do before you start teambuilding or before a team review.

### Instructions

Please answer each item as carefully and as accurately as you can by awarding the team points out of five on the following items (one is low, five is high).

1 We are all convinced of the value of teamwork.
2 We are realistic in our expectations of one another.
3 We are working on improving our teamwork.
4 Team meetings are marked by creative discussion.
5 Relationships with others (individuals and groups) outside the team are good.
6 We enjoy one another's company.
7 We understand and can accept our own and each other's backgrounds, expectations and assumptions.
8 All the members are committed to the team.
9 We are aware of what causes one another stress, and how to help with this.
10 There is good communication between us.

11 Conflict is acceptable and is not denied.
12 We are able to resolve conflict between team members.
13 We understand and accept one another's personalities.
14 We tend to complement rather than compete with each other.
15 We are aware of and value one another's gifts and competences.
16 We understand our natural roles within the team.
17 Most of us are functioning in our most appropriate role.
18 Leadership of the team is respected and followed.
19 The team authority structure is clear.
20 We each know what the team goals are and they are realistic.
21 Each of us is clear as to his or her own tasks.
22 Decision making is shared.
23 We review the team's progress and objectives regularly.
24 There are opportunities for training and personal growth.
25 We have adequate spiritual fellowship.

## Interpreting the team satisfaction questionnaire

A score of 100 or more suggests satisfactory teamwork. You may want to consider the items highlighted by a score of three or less. Perhaps you can discuss these together to try to find ways of increasing your teamwork satisfaction.

A score of less than 70 suggests that your satisfaction is so low that it may be affecting your performance and even your health (unless you are an exceptional stoic!). It would be helpful to discuss these things through with someone outside the team and try to get some objectivity before involving fellow team members in the discussion.

**Warning** A working group may well score less on this scale since it is not a team and therefore could not be expected to have all the team attributes operating. Copyright © Gordon and Rosemary Jones, 1993. Published by Hatters Lane Publications, 196 Hatters Lane, High Wycombe, Bucks HP13 7LY.

# Exercise 6

## HOW TO BUILD A GENOGRAM

A genogram is a map of your relationship experiences. It is best done in conjunction with Chapter 4. You may start building a genogram by drawing your family tree, including all those people with whom you had a significant relationship in childhood. This may mean including friends and neighbours, even the family pet!

Building a genogram is best done in dialogue with another member of your team. If you are a small team, you can all work together, each member developing his or her own genogram in turn, as the others elicit information. This should give considerable scope for you to understand one another better.

The following are some issues you might consider in order to determine how you related to and felt about those who were significant to you in your childhood and adolescence, and how to put them in on your genogram. If you can draw, you could add drawings and diagrams (see example below).

Start by asking one another some or all of the following questions:

1 Strength of relationship   Whom do you think of first?
                             Who means most to you?

2 Warmth                     Who showed you warmth?
3 Acceptance                 Who accepted you? Who

| | was reliable? |
|---|---|
| 4 Rejection | Who rejected you? Who let you down? |
| 5 Trust | Whom could/do you trust? Who trusted you? |
| 6 Fun | What was fun? With whom did you have fun? |
| 7 Anxiety/fear | Who or what caused you anxiety or fear? |
| 8 Control | Who controlled whom? And how? Who controlled you? Whom did you control and how? |
| 9 Decisions | How were decisions made? |
| 10 Directness | Was there confrontation? |
| 11 Communication | Was there open communication? Between whom? |
| 12 Secrets | Were there things that were not talked about? |
| 13 Loss or desertion | Any patterns through generations? |
| 14 Finances | What was the meaning of wealth? (see also question 8 above) |
| 15 Stability | Did you move house a lot? Were relationships stable? Who provided stability? |
| 16 Male/female roles | Were they flexible or stereo-typical? |
| 17 Punishment | How were you punished? What was it like? |
| 18 Conflict | What kind of conflict was there? How was it resolved? |
| 19 Feelings | Were feelings shown or covered up? |

|    |    |    |
|----|----|----|
| 20 | Socialisation | What kind of feelings were acceptable?<br>Did people get together?<br>What was it like?<br>Were you included? If so what role did you play? |
| 21 | Barriers/separation | Between whom were there barriers?<br>What kind of barriers? |
| 22 | Your 'style' | How did you handle tension?<br>How did you get attention? |
| 23 | Rules, taboos | What unwritten rules were there? |
| 24 | Absences | Was anyone away a significant amount? |
| 25 | Freedom of choice | Was autonomy encouraged?<br>Was it OK to be different? |
| 26 | Sickness | What were people's attitudes to illness?<br>What was the mood when someone was sick? |

## EXAMPLE – RUTH'S GENOGRAM

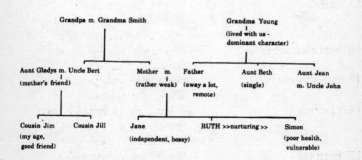

Ruth says, 'I resent bossy women – both my older sister and my grandmother told me what to do all the time. I tend to rescue people and like nurturing them. My good friendship with Jim and close relationship with my brother Simon have helped me to relate well with peer group males.'

Adapted from material prepared by the late David Meech, Wycliffe Bible Translators. Copyright © Gordon and Rosemary Jones, 1993. Published by Hatters Lane Publications, 196 Hatters Lane, High Wycombe, Bucks HP13 7LY.

# Exercise 7

## SIMILARITIES GRID

This grid could be used in conjunction with Chapter 4, which is about expectations and assumptions, as it is helpful in identifying differences in people and thus aiding their understanding of one another. It also enables people who are in a minority to explain their feelings. The dissimilarities between team members can be a potential problem area and yet those same dissimilarities can also help strengthen teamwork.

The grid below is adapted from a grid that we constructed when we were teambuilding with a five person team working in a third world country.

**Parameters**

1 Married (ma) or single (s)
2 Female (f) or male (m)
3 English (em) or non-English (n) mother tongue
4 European (Eu) or American (A)
5 New worker (w) or established worker (ww)
6 Extravert (E) or Introvert (I)
7 Senser (S) or Intuitive (N)
8 Feeler (F) or Thinker (T)
9 Perceiver (P) or Judger (J)
10 Age 20–35 (a) 36–50 (b) 51–70 (c)

| Name | 1 | 2 | 3 | 4 | 5 | 6 | 7 | 8 | 9 | 10 |
|------|---|---|---|---|---|---|---|---|---|----|
| Helga | s | f | n | Eu | ww | E | S | F | P | b |
| Arthur | ma | m | em | A | ww | I | N | F | P | b |
| Gunilla | s | f | n | Eu | w | I | S | T | J | a |
| Tanya | s | f | n | Eu | w | I | N | T | J | a |
| Mary | s | f | em | Eu | w | I | N | F | J | b |

The new members (Gunilla, Tanya, Mary) felt they had little to offer to the team because of their lack of experience. The experienced members did not feel this way about them, as the new members had more recently received formal training. The more experienced ones were looking forward to tapping into this knowledge.

Arthur was concerned that he was the only married male team member. The implications of this were discussed. Apart from being the only married man on the team, Arthur was the only American. However, he was an introvert in a predominantly introvert team and a mother tongue English speaker in a team using English as the language of communication.

Helga, the leader was, like most of the team, a single lady. She was the only extravert on the team and shared only with Gunilla her preference for sensing and only with Arthur her preference for making perceptive judgments, using the Myers Briggs terminology.

The new members were all judgers (liking a planned and ordered lifestyle) and were facing a totally unknown experience. They felt they wanted to know more of what was facing them. Helga and Arthur, as perceptives (liking a flexible, spontaneous lifestyle), tended to leave decision making until it was absolutely necessary.

Copyright © Gordon and Rosemary Jones, 1993. Published by Hatters Lane Publications, 196 Hatters Lane, High Wycombe, Bucks HP13 7LY.

# Exercise 8

## INTEREST THEMES

This exercise will help you determine your gifts. It is best done in conjunction with Chapter 9 on gifts and abilities.

### Instructions

Read through the following theme descriptions and award yourself points out of ten against each theme, according to the degree to which matches your interest preferences. Ask a friend or relative if they agree with your estimates. Please note that these descriptions list *likely* behaviour, attributes, occupations, etc. None of us match one type exactly.

Realistic – R Theme – These people need to see tangible results from their work. They prefer to work outside, with tools, machines or animals. They prefer to work with things rather than with people or ideas. They may be described as honest, straight-talking, practical, modest, frugal, conforming. They may find difficulty in expressing their feelings and in verbal communication. They are often found in military or emergency services, agricultural and mechanical, skilled trade and building environments. People in typical Realistic occupations are farmers, mechanics, carpenters, police officers, foresters and general maintenance people.

Investigative – I Theme – These people thirst after knowledge. They want to understand the world about them and study theoretical systems such as biology, physics, mathematics, etc. They may be described as precise, independent, intellectually curious, analytical, quiet, reserved and logical. They enjoy solving abstract problems and facing ambiguous challenges. They prefer thinking to doing, are often seen as 'freethinkers', and are uncomfortable with rules and regulations. They are found in mathematical, scientific, research, medical technology and problem solving environments. People in typical Investigative occupations are computer programmers, maths lecturers, biologists and pharmacists.

Artistic – A Theme – These people like to express their individuality. This leads to creativity in the arts (drama, painting, music, writing) and/or in concepts and ideas (architecture). They may be described as idealistic, expressive, dissenting, impetuous, temperamental, complex and creative. They have little interest in the business and commercial world and are often unconventional in dress and lifestyle. They are often found in performing/entertaining, arts/crafts and highly original environments. People in typical Artistic occupations are commercial artists, musicians, photographers, actors and journalists.

Social – S Theme – These people need to help other people. They often have naturally empathetic skills demonstrated in listening and understanding other people. They seek to nurture, heal and promote growth and wholeness in others. They may be described as sociable, considerate, patient, caring, sympathetic, generous, responsible and cheerful. Their preferred way of solving problems is by discussion with others, and they are able to handle their own relationships and those between others. They are usually uncomfortable with machines. They are often found in educational, welfare, humanitarian and medical service environments. People in typical Social occupations are social workers, nurses, primary teachers, counsellors and pastors.

Enterprising – E Theme – These people need to persuade other people to their point of view. This means they are usually effective in selling, leadership, and public speaking. They may be described as industrious, dominant, self-confident, ambitious, influential, in-the-limelight, well-liked and optimistic. They can be impatient with theoretical or detailed work. They like the trappings of authority (status, power, wealth). They are often found in promotional, political, merchandising and business management environments. People in typical Enterprising occupations are estate agents, retail sales managers, marketing directors, union negotiators and management consultants.

Conventional – C Theme – These people need structure and order. Where these exist they keep to procedures and organisational rules. Where these don't exist they will bring order and system to their environment. They may be described as stable, cautious, systematic, dogged, fastidious, reliable and accurate. They are less interested in individuality than in corporate responsibility. They dislike ambiguity, preferring to know exactly what is required of them. They are often found in office, financial and procedural environments. People in typical Conventional occupations are secretaries, book-keepers, VDU operators and accountants.

**Example**

| Theme | – | R | I | A | S | E | C |
|---|---|---|---|---|---|---|---|
| Self estimate | – | 8 | 6 | 2 | 3 | 4 | 5 |
| Friend's estimate | – | 7 | 7 | 3 | 4 | 5 | 6 |
| Relative's estimate | – | 9 | 7 | 4 | 2 | 4 | 6 |
| Total score | – | 24 | 20 | 9 | 9 | 13 | 17 |

My Interest Themes R I C

Copyright © Gordon and Rosemary Jones, 1991. Adapted from *Naturally Gifted*, Chapter 3 (see Resource section).

# Exercise 9

## TEAM ROLES – SELF-PERCEPTION INVENTORY

This exercise is linked to Chapter 10 on team roles. It is best to do it before reading Chapter 10.

### Instructions

For each section allocate a total of ten points to the sentences which you think best describe your behaviour. These points may be distributed among several sentences: in extreme cases they might be spread among all the sentences or ten points may be given to a single sentence. Enter the points in the table on p 188.

I What I believe I can contribute to the team:
   a) I can quickly see the advantage of new opportunities.
   b) I can work well with a very wide range of people.
   c) The ability to produce ideas is one of my natural assets.
   d) My ability rests in being able to draw people out whenever I detect they have something of value to contribute to the group objectives.
   e) My capacity to follow through has much to do with my personal effectiveness.
   f) I am ready to face temporary unpopularity if it leads to worthwhile results in the end.
   g) I am quick to sense what is likely to work in a situation with which I am familiar.

h) I can offer a reasoned case for alternative courses of action without introducing bias or prejudice.

II If I have a possible shortcoming in teamwork, it could be that:
   a) I am not at ease unless meetings are well-structured and controlled and generally well-conducted.
   b) I am inclined to be too generous towards others who have a valid viewpoint that has not been given a proper airing.
   c) I have a tendency to talk a lot once the group gets on to new ideas.
   d) My objective outlook makes it difficult for me to join in readily and enthusiastically with colleagues.
   e) I am sometimes seen as forceful and authoritarian if there is a need to get something done.
   f) I find it difficult to lead from the front, perhaps because I am over-responsive to group atmosphere.
   g) I am apt to get too caught up in ideas that occur to me and so lose track of what is happening.
   h) My colleagues tend to see me as worrying unnecessarily over detail and the possibility that things may go wrong.

III When involved in a project with other people:
   a) I have an aptitude for influencing people without pressuring them.
   b) My general vigilance prevents careless mistakes and omissions.
   c) I am ready to press for action to make sure that the meeting does not waste time or lose sight of the main objective.
   d) I can be counted on to contribute something original.
   e) I am always ready to back a good suggestion in the common interest.
   f) I am keen to look for the latest in new ideas and developments.
   g) I believe my capacity for cool judgment is appreciated by others.

    h) I can be relied upon to see that all essential work is organised.

IV My characteristic approach to group work is that:
    a) I have a quiet interest in getting to know colleagues better.
    b) I am not reluctant to challenge the views of others or to hold a minority view myself.
    c) I can usually find a line of argument to refute unsound propositions.
    d) I think I have a talent for making things work once a plan has to be put into operation.
    e) I have a tendency to avoid the obvious and to come out with the unexpected.
    f) I bring a touch of perfectionism to any team job I undertake.
    g) I am ready to make use of contacts outside the group itself.
    h) While I am interested in all views I have no hesitation in making up my mind once a decision has to be made.

V I gain satisfaction in a job because:
    a) I enjoy analysing situations and weighing up all the possible choices.
    b) I am interested in finding practical solutions to problems.
    c) I like to feel I am fostering good working relationships.
    d) I can have a strong influence on decisions.
    e) I can meet people who may have something new to offer.
    f) I can get people to agree on a necessary course of action.
    g) I feel in my element where I can give a task my full attention.
    h) I like to find a field that stretches my imagination.

VI If I were suddenly given a difficult task with limited time and unfamiliar people:

a) I would feel like retiring to a corner to devise a way out of the impasse before developing a line.

b) I would be ready to work with whoever showed the most positive approach, however difficult he might be.

c) I would find some way of reducing the size of the task by establishing what different individuals might best contribute.

d) My natural sense of urgency would help to ensure that we did not fall behind schedule.

e) I believe I would keep cool and maintain my capacity to think straight.

f) I would retain a steadiness of purpose in spite of the pressures.

g) I would be prepared to take a positive lead if I felt the group was making no progress.

h) I would open up discussions with a view to stimulating new thoughts and getting something moving.

VII With reference to the problems to which I am subject in working in groups:

a) I am apt to show my impatience with those who are obstructing progress.

b) Others may criticise me for being too analytical and insufficiently intuitive.

c) My desire to ensure that work is properly done can hold up proceedings.

d) I tend to get bored easily and rely on one or two stimulating members to spark me off.

e) I find it difficult to start unless goals are clear.

f) I am sometimes poor at explaining and clarifying complex points that occur to me.

g) I am conscious of demanding from others the things I cannot do myself.

h) I hestitate to get my points across when I run up against real opposition.

# POINTS TABLE FOR SELF-PERCEPTION INVENTORY

|  | ITEM | | | | | | | |
|---|---|---|---|---|---|---|---|---|
| SECTION | a | b | c | c | e | f | g | h |
| I | | | | | | | | |
| II | | | | | | | | |
| III | | | | | | | | |
| IV | | | | | | | | |
| V | | | | | | | | |
| VI | | | | | | | | |
| VII | | | | | | | | |

To interpret the self-perception inventory you should now look at the analysis sheet below.

## Self-perception inventory analysis sheet

Transpose the scores taken from the points table above, entering them section by section in the table below. Then add up the points in each column to give a total team role distribution score.

| SECTION | Imp | Co | Sh | Pl | RI | ME | TW | Com |
|---------|-----|-----|-----|-----|-----|-----|-----|-----|
| I | g | d | f | c | a | h | b | e |
| II | a | b | e | g | c | d | f | h |
| III | h | a | c | d | f | g | e | b |
| IV | d | h | b | e | g | c | a | f |
| V | b | f | d | h | e | a | c | g |
| VI | f | c | g | a | h | e | b | d |
| VII | e | g | a | f | d | b | h | c |
| Total | | | | | | | | |

Imp = Implementer      Co = Coordinator      Sh = Shaper
Pl = Plant      RI = Resource Investigator      ME = Monitor Evaluator
TW = Team Worker      Com = Completer

The self-perception inventory was developed as part of a government funded research programme by Dr Meredith Belbin, in conjunction with The Management College, Henley.

## How to interpret your scores

The highest score indicates your preferred role in the team. The next highest scores suggest possible team roles which you could adopt if there is less need for you to adopt your preferred team role.

The two lowest scores indicate your possible areas of weakness. You are not likely to be able to function well in these roles, and they are better filled by team members with strengths complementary to yours.

# Exercise 10

## TEAM LEADERSHIP SKILLS RATING

How good at team leadership are you? How well do you know your own strengths and weaknesses? This exercise should help you determine this. It is best done in conjunction with Chapter 11, which is about team leadership.

(This test was developed by Steve Chalke, and printed in *Alpha* magazine, Elm House Christian Publications, November 1992.)

### Instructions

Score three if you consider yourself strong; two if you perform averagely; one if you are a bit weak; nought if you are hopeless and you know it.

Give a photocopy of this questionnaire (before you have filled it in) to another leader in your church who knows you well and get him or her to complete it while you are not around.

Get your fellow leader to return his or her copy and then compare your results.

1 I give team members a sense of ownership by involving them in goal setting for our work.

2 We have regular team meetings to assess our progress.

3 I place high priority on listening to the ideas and views of team members.

4 I provide opportunities for open discussion of problems to encourage the finding of solutions.

5 I am willing to change my mind.

6 My team members work well together because they know what is expected of them in terms of both standards and tasks.

7 My team knows that I trust and respect it.

8 My team members know that I appreciate the work they do.

9 I regularly give praise and recognition publicly to individuals for their achievements.

10 I regularly give recognition privately to individuals for their achievements.

11 I understand that conflict within teams is normal, but work to resolve it quickly before it becomes destructive.

12 I'm good at spotting talent and ability in others.

13 I find it easy to delegate authority.

14 I work hard to provide opportunities that will stretch and challenge team members and help them develop new skills.

15 I discuss a team member's performance with him at least every six months.

16 I ensure that team members have access to necessary training to do their job effectively.

17 I am willing to confront sensitively problems and differences of opinion with the team.

18 I am willing to replace team members who cannot or will not meet reasonable standards after appropriate training.

19 I talk with team members honestly and openly, and encourage the same kind of communication in return.

20 I have a good personal relationship with my team members.

21 I lead by setting high standards and a good example.

22 I keep agreements with team members because their trust is essential to my leadership.

23 I have a good track record for keeping volunteer team members.

24 My team members find the experience of working with me enjoyable and fulfilling.
25 I enjoy working with othcr people.

## What does your team leadership skills rating mean?

**65+** You are a skilled team leader, though there is room for improvement. You have the kind of positive attitude towards other people that is essential in order to build and maintain a strong team. Before congratulating yourself too heartily, you would be wise to get the results of your friend's objective assessment of your skills.

**50–64** You have an acceptable team leadership rating which means that with a bit of hard work and discipline, effective teambuilding is within your grasp.

**30–49** If you have given yourself and your friend has given you a team leadership rating in this bracket, it's time you did some very serious thinking about the way in which you handle other people. It's up to you to make a determined effort.

**Less than 30** Don't despair; team leadership skills can be learned. How did your friend score you? Maybe you are just too humble! But if you both scored you around the same mark, very urgent action is needed. Buy a book on team leadership/management skills and read it today!